UpsideDown
Leadership

Also by Michael C. Blackwell

New Millennium Families

A Place For Miracles

UpsideDown Leadership

A Dozen Big Ideas
To Turn Your Nonprofit Organization
Right Side Up

Michael C. Blackwell

2003
Parkway Publishers, Inc.
Boone, North Carolina

Copyright © 2003 by Michael C. Blackwell
All Rights Reserved

Library of Congress Cataloging-in-Publication Data

Blackwell, Michael C.
  Upsidedown leadership : a dozen big ideas to turn your nonprofit organization right side up / Michael C. Blackwell.
    p. cm.
  ISBN 1-887905-71-5
    1. Nonprofit organizations--Management. I. Title.

  HD62.6 .B57 2003
  658.4'092--dc21   2002155601

Jacket and book design:
Jim Edminson/BCH Communications

Dedication

To *Gabriella*...

my granddaughter,
who was born July 15, 2000, and gave me
new hope, new light, new purpose.

Contents

Acknowledgments

Introduction

Chapter 1: .... *page 1*
Your organizational mirror should reflect your face

Chapter 2: .... *page 11*
Choosing to lead is committing to prepare

Chapter 3: .... *page 22*
There's no juice in a steamrolled tomato

Chapter 4: .... *page 27*
Embrace your staff at arm's length

Chapter 5: .... *page 35*
Learn the culture before it eats you

Chapter 6: .... *page 47*
Survive your political jungle

Chapter 7: .... *page 61*
Command your political jungle

Chapter 8: .... *page 71*
Embrace change as you would a rich uncle

Chapter 9: .... *page 81*
When change follows you home, claim it

Chapter 10: .... *page 91*
Mine support like a joy geologist

Chapter 11: .... *page 103*
Leadership by the numbers

Chapter 12: .... *page 119*
TAP the MVP within you

Conclusion

Acknowledgments

I could not have written this book without the valuable help of Norman Jameson and Jennie Counts. These two insightful colleagues have labored with me over every word, concept, and principle in *UpsideDown Leadership*.

After working alongside me for 12 years, Norman Jameson became a consultant and creative entrepreneur. In my opinion, his way with words is outstanding. He encouraged me for years to write a book on leadership for nonprofit organizations. His persistence and assistance are evident on every page.

Jennie Counts is executive vice president (administration) for Baptist Children's Homes of North Carolina. She brought a freshness and zeal to this project over the many months of organizing, writing, and re-writing. I am grateful to her for the hours she spent with Norman and me to give form and substance to the leadership principles she has heard me espouse since 1987.

W. James Edminson, director of communications for Baptist Children's Homes of North Carolina, is responsible for the design of the book, including the cover. Jim's creative genius has brought a lively sense of fun to the project.

Grateful appreciation is also extended to the Broyhill Family Foundation, Lenoir, NC, for their support of this project.

Michael C. Blackwell
Thomasville, North Carolina 27361-0338

*A board gives you
the position of leader. You earn
the authority to lead when you value
your staff and make decisions that
support them.*

Introduction

LEADERSHIP IS PERSONAL

∼ In the opening episode of the Emmy Award winning, 10-hour television drama "Band of Brothers," Captain Sobel worked, drove, threatened, cajoled and brutalized the men of Easy Company until they formed the best unit in the 101st Airborne Division. His sole task was to prepare these men to parachute behind World War II enemy lines, where their lives would be at great risk. They would engage the enemy with minimal firepower, separated from supply lines in unfamiliar territory.

Their assignment was ominous but clear. When Sobel was done with them, the men of Easy Company could run farther, sprint faster, shoot straighter and fight harder than every other unit. He could prepare them physically; however, he could not lead them. He didn't embody the leadership traits that inspired them to follow.

In fact, the company's noncommissioned officers put their careers on the line, and risked being court-martialed and shot rather than follow Captain Sobel into battle. Unanimously, they appealed to their general, who reprimanded them and threw them out, vowing that in different circumstances he would have had them shot for treason.

Then the general quietly replaced Captain Sobel.

Sobel, who longed to lead men into battle, learned the life-and-death difference between positional leadership and earned leadership. He led his company in training because he wore captain's bars on his collar. He could never lead his company into battle because his men knew that Sobel's rank would not protect them from his incompetence, ignorance, indecisiveness and self-doubt.

When it was only training, when lives were not on the line, Sobel's men "let" him lead them. They obeyed him, but they did not respect or trust him.

Good leaders don't have to be liked. We waste a lot of time and effort trying to be liked. But to truly lead, the person who holds the position of leadership must earn the respect and trust of those who would follow.

You know that. The question is, how?

You've been selected for a position of leadership in your organization. Suddenly, it's in your hands. You have to meet the budget; find, train and retain the quality staff that will make your job possible; fulfill the mission; address your many publics; keep the staff, directors, donors and clients happy; make sure your organization meets all the

Introduction

government requirements for licensing and accreditation; make sure the grass is mowed and the flower gardens weeded for the big alumni weekend; and, at the same time, keep yourself fresh, innovative, challenged, charged and excited.

But deep down, you really long simply to implement your vision for your organization. How do you earn the authority of your position as president or executive director or CEO so that your staff and board will follow your lead?

Here are some ideas.

The ideas contained herein were not created for this book, but are truths discovered through decades of nonprofit leadership, most significantly in a statewide system of residential child care, in churches and in political groups, all working – as nonprofits do – to make the world a better place and to lessen the burden for those least able to handle the load themselves.

Whether you are the CEO, president or director, or whether you are a staff member, board member or employee wanting to be the best in your area of responsibility, these ideas will help you. In helping you, they will help those you serve. For that, I am grateful.

UpsideDown
Leadership

#1

THE BIG IDEA

Your organization needs a face – yours.

Chapter One

YOUR ORGANIZATIONAL MIRROR SHOULD REFLECT YOUR FACE

∼ When I came to lead the Baptist Children's Homes of North Carolina in 1983, the board pinned me with the positional leadership rank of president. I was the leader because the board said I was the leader.

But I knew instinctively that if the authority of my leadership did not extend beyond position, I could never lead the organization through the difficult days it faced. Like many old, established nonprofits, ours was dependent upon a century-old vision, and it had lost momentum in recent decades. It needed a fresh vision, a new energy. It needed a new inspiration and allegiance that required trust in leadership.

At the time Baptist Children's Homes had approximately 280 employees, from managers to supervisors, to residential counselors to farm workers and maintenance staff members. These personnel operated from campuses and group homes in 11 locations that stretched 400 miles apart. During the first few months of my administration, I scheduled a half-hour uninterrupted talk with each staff member. They interviewed me as much as I interviewed them. I gave them a chance to know me, to hear my vision, to peek behind the veil of leadership and see the man.

At the same time, they established their own identity in my mind, and every decision I've made since has been with the knowledge of our staff members as workers, husbands, children, wives, laity, hobbyists, civic leaders, volunteers, actors, gardeners – as individuals.

Individuals have a face that tells everyone they meet much about who they are. Your organization needs a face. As the leader, you are the identity, the personification of your organization. I am not Baptist Children's Homes. But I have worked hard to become the face of BCH, so that whenever people see this face, hear this voice, they think Baptist Children's Homes and how we help hurting children and heal broken families.

One day at our wilderness camping facility, we were lining up leadership for a capital campaign. One of the volunteers asked innocently enough why my name appeared on all the campaign materials. "You may leave someday," he said. "Then all this material will be outdated."

Your name is your commitment to the organization. An institution eventually becomes the lengthened shadow of its CEO. I want the face and heart tug of Baptist Children's Homes to be the face of a child. But the public arena, marketplace face has to be that of the CEO.

The face of Focus on the Family is James Dobson, not an anonymous family. The face of Samaritan's Purse is Franklin Graham. The face of Habitat for Humanity is Millard Fuller.

Who is the face of your organization? Is it hard for you? Do you delegate that responsibility, sending a subordinate to represent you and the agency? If so, that sends a diffused message about leadership.

How do you begin to establish yourself as the "face" of your organization? Remember, there is no insignificant event, no meaningless public appearance whether you are speaking to one potential donor or a stadium full of rabid fans.

I get to meetings early to get a sense of the crowd. I want to become a familiar face before the face utters a word. I'm fooling myself if I think that everyone knows who I am. Even if I've spoken to that church congregation or civic club a dozen times before, I do not assume that everyone knows me. That would be delusional.

When you're there early, meet the people before you speak to them. Get unrehearsed examples; learn some names you can throw out during your address. It's an important way of connecting. If you're an introvert and that kind of "working the crowd" is hard for you, get over it. Personality is outgoing.

No one worked a crowd better than Strom Thurmond, active in the Senate until age 100. I once followed him into a hotel in Charleston, S.C., and he shook hands with every person, from bellhop to maid. He held their hands, looked them in the eye for that instant shorter than a "Hello, how are you?" but long enough for each recipient momentarily to feel he was the only person in the room with Thurmond. In the meantime, in my state of North Carolina, a candidate for governor got squashed because, among other things, he didn't know how to shake hands. He touched every hand, but he didn't catch any eye.

Sometimes pastors don't take pains to know every name in their congregation. Get a name. Call their name. Recognize them. They're your people. If you don't call their names, you act like you don't even like them, and they will one day rise up and get you.

I'm bugged when several staff members from the same organization attend a function and cluster among themselves. They're not consciously representing the organization among the people. If they don't put themselves forward because they're not wearing the mantle of leadership, it's likely that mantle will never fall on their shoulders.

The CEO has to work hard to become the institution's face. It's not a task for the faint-hearted; it's

Your organizational mirror...

exhausting work. Even when you don't feel like being "the face," you have to put on the face and be the face. If you're dog-tired, don't drag. If you're pooped, you can't be short-tempered. If you're upset, smile. Whatever baggage, troubles and trials occupied your mind on the way to your public appearance, tuck them away. This audience doesn't want to know that. This audience wants to hear from you how well your organization is doing, how many people you serve and how they can help you.

I am by nature an extrovert. Yet, I tire working a crowd. But when I step behind the podium, they don't know it. I find the energy, sound the notes and make music. I'll rest in the car on the way home. In fact, I may collapse in the car and take five minutes of recuperation time even before I turn the key, but when I'm "on," I find the energy to be the face of BCH.

When an issue that your agency deals with becomes headline news for some reason, do media representatives call you for your comment? Do you shun the media, or cultivate them? When there is an issue on the public lip that relates to children and families, child abuse, day care, residential child care, teenager malaise, I want part of that conversation. I want the public to hear in the newspaper or on the radio or television the Baptist Children's Homes leader's perspective on that issue.

Why? Because I want my picture in the paper?

No, because I want the face of Baptist Children's Homes in the news, giving an informed perspective, reminding people that BCH is on the job, serving children and families, and, by the way, we could always use your help.

That doesn't happen if you shirk the media, if you never write an "expert" column for submission, if you never call the editor just to introduce yourself to him or her. You don't have time? When the bad news hits and you're meeting the editor for the very first time in a hostile, combative mood, will you wish you had made time then?

It doesn't always work. Despite the fact that we printed our monthly newsletter at a nearby newspaper, and I'd done my homework, and our communications department had an excellent relationship with the staff, we were the victims of a scurrilous story by that newspaper. Two young reporters smelled "prize story" when a disgruntled employee went to the paper with allegations about the quality of care we provided, the kind of children we served and the qualifications of the staff who served them. The resultant story precipitated one of the most difficult weeks of my life. But we did things right and got past it. The incident provided an essential lesson on being the face of the institution. That is, you have to be the face to your employees, as well – the calm, reassuring face that tells them their leader is on the job, working to

Your organizational mirror...

make things be "all right." That's what a leader does. He makes things all right.

Our employees and the children in our care were devastated by that story. So I was in with the staff the next morning. I reassured them, heard them, let them vent, and then told them by my presence that I was on top of things. We kept our trustees informed and relayed to the staff their trustee support. We scheduled visits to all the cottages where our children live to calm and reassure them. I held children while they cried and listened to the staff while they expressed anger and betrayal. We quickly fashioned a public response. In the end we discerned no long-term negative effects.

The long-term message for a leader, though, is that to have the authority of leadership in crisis, you must be seen by your people. They want to see you on the job, not as the Wizard of Oz pulling levers from behind a curtain.

That dilemma faced President Bush on Sept. 11, 2001. Following the terrorist attacks in New York and Washington, Bush followed the written plan, got airborne on Air Force One, and flew to fortified bunkers in the Midwest. While the wisdom of that action was voiced by news commentators, the people still swallowed hard, furrowed their concerned brows and said, "Where's the president?" It's not that we didn't know where he was. We knew where he was. But we wanted to see him.

We wanted to see our leader, to see his face.

We have to know the leader is going to take charge. We had minute-by-minute television reports, but we wanted minute-by-minute directions from our boss. When the crisis comes, the leader will take hold, whatever that means. People want to know that.

When New York Mayor Rudy Giuliani's way to the World Trade Center was blocked, he found another way around. He knew how important it was to his city that he be there. What could he do? Save someone? No, but there were still eight million people and a nation who needed to be assured that they would be okay. Presence equals assurance.

In 1999, North Carolina endured some terrible flooding as a result of Hurricane Floyd. Our easternmost campus was under three feet of water. To get there, I would have had to drive 175 miles into horrible weather. I decided to let the director of that facility be the leadership face on the scene, and I stayed in Thomasville, where we evacuated the children from the eastern campus. When the vans arrived, I was there to greet them, to reassure the staff and children that, except for the weather, everything else was under control.

On-site in the east later, I helped clean the flooded house of one of our least visible workers. I introduced myself, and he said, "I know who you are." Some weeks later, at a rally of that campus's employees, the man exclaimed how I had helped him shovel mud out of his house. He was still shaking his head over what had been a spontaneous act on my part.

Yours is the face of your organization. Make sure people see it.

#2

THE BIG IDEA

*Use tools available to help you uncover
the leader within you.*

Chapter Two

CHOOSING TO LEAD IS COMMITTING TO PREPARE

~ Stephen Covey says that leadership is a choice, not a position. You may think that you're a leader, you may wear the rank of leader on your collar or your corner office or your parking spot. But if your company of people, your organization of professionals, your staff doesn't view you as a leader – you're not.

If you're in a position as leader but carry no authority of leadership, you know it. You feel it. You sense it. You see how people respond to you, how your ideas fall flat with no enthusiasm from those you're trying to inspire. People leave your meetings laden with notes and instructions, and a few days later you realize that nothing has been done. Staff members treat your directives as suggestions. Donors and board members don't return your calls.

Are you brave enough to learn how your staff views you? It can be done in quantifiable, scientific ways. I've done it several times, and it hurts like a gut kick. But negative feedback is the only truly helpful, educational feedback. You like the strokes of positive feedback, but how does it help you change a weakness?

"Would that we had the gift that God would give us, that we could see ourselves as others see us," wrote poet Robert Burns.

How can you know how your staff sees you, and measure how they see you as leader? One of my mantras is, "School is never out for the professional." We're fortunate in North Carolina to have many avenues through which to pursue personal-growth education. Two of the best are the Center for Creative Leadership, with offices in Greensboro and in Colorado Springs, Colorado; and the University of North Carolina School of Business Administration. I've also done quality work with Bell Leadership in Chapel Hill; an 11-day introspective with LifeWay Christian Resources (formerly the Southern Baptist Sunday School Board), an Outward Bound-type executive development event, and an intensive self-evaluation through a sabbatical.

Some of the instruments used in these places for staff and self-evaluation include:

- The Learning Tactics Inventory
    (Jossey-Bass/Pfeiffer)
- Job Challenge Profile
    (Jossey-Bass/Pfeiffer)
- Thomas-Kilmann Conflict Mode Instrument
    (Consulting Psychologists Press)

- Skillscope for Managers
  (Center for Creative Leadership)
- Change Style Indicator
  (Discovery Learning Press)
- Firo-B (Consulting Psychologists Press)

Utilizing the feedback instruments means asking your staff members, anonymously, to evaluate you. They fill out a form that gives a quantifiable measure of how they view your leadership skills and personality. They're asked to list your strengths and weaknesses. You may not have a clue as to what they view as your weaknesses. You may be relieved to learn that they are completely aware of the weakness you thought you were so skillfully hiding. After their evaluation, you won't have to waste so much energy trying to hide it, and instead, can put that energy to work overcoming it!

You want to put yourself through these things for self-awareness, which is one of the real keys of leadership. How well do you know yourself? Without such an effort, you're really blind to how you're perceived.

Sometimes that blindness is the comforting bliss of ignorance, and when you take the tests and submit yourself to evaluation, it can be devastating.

I once had one of my managers go through it, giving his staff a chance to evaluate him anonymously. He learned that his leadership was by position only, and he had earned no authority with his staff whatsoever. His staff felt he did not respect them, nor value them, nor pay any attention to them. He could not make a decision, but he also made them feel that he totally disregarded any idea they had. It devastated him to learn these things, and it led to a negotiated early retirement.

PREPARING TO LEAD

What can someone who wants to be a leader do to prepare for such a responsibility? Honestly, much of gaining a leadership position is time and place. You're in the right place in your life. You know the right people. You've done the grunt work in an area you love and in which you excel. Something opens, and there you are.

People wonder when the mantle will fall on them. When will they get a chance to lead? What if it never comes? My ego would make me think there is something out there on a larger stage for which I could be tapped. But am I willing to go out and work to do anything different from what I'm doing now?

Winston Churchill is a prime 20th century example of a person who was thrust into the vortex of events that combined with his personality and preparation to make him a leader for the ages. The great 19th century example is Abraham Lincoln. The great 18th century example is George Washington.

Lyndon Johnson, one of greatest Senate majority leaders ever, was propelled to international lead-

Choosing to lead...

ership by President Kennedy's assassination.

CBS news anchor Dan Rather's career was "made" by Kennedy's death. He broke the story and rode it for days into the national consciousness. In a sense, his career took off at age 32. He admits that journalists dream of such a story. Did he prepare for the mantle he wears as one of the most respected national figures in America? Definitely. He studied, practiced, took the hard assignments and networked. When the position of leadership opened, he was a natural choice. Sometimes, his friendly competitor Tom Brokaw says, "Leadership just reaches down and taps you on the shoulder."

Sometimes you have the lucky break. The 1974 Pulitzer Prize winner for spot news photography was sitting in his car at a Beverly Hills shopping center when a man the next row over pushed a woman into her car and tried to drive off with her. She had the panicked presence of mind to keep rolling out the other side. She fell onto the cement, and he came out after her with a knife. The ensuing struggle before the assailant was shot produced the prize-winning series of photos. But Anthony Roberts never accepted the notion that he just happened to be "in the right spot." He got the pictures because he was ready, he said. He was prepared, trained, alert and brave enough to step into the fray.

As an aside, Roberts' winning series did not include what would have been the most dramatic picture, that of a policeman shooting the assailant to keep him from stabbing the woman. Roberts had put down his camera to help the woman – a decision he never regretted.

In 1995, an amateur won the Pulitzer Prize for his picture of a fireman carrying a baby out of the burning rubble of the Murrah Federal Building in Oklahoma City. Time, place and readiness.

I didn't think that George W. Bush was prepared to be president. But he wears the mantle well. After Sept. 11, 2001, he grew quickly into the position and he is the president. Not every president, sadly, has grown into the position. Think of Andrew Johnson who followed Abraham Lincoln and came within one vote of being convicted of impeachment.

Harry Truman became a good leader, a very decisive leader. Although unprepared to become president, he was propelled into that position by Franklin Roosevelt's death. Some can assume the mantle, and some can't. Even as deified as Ronald Reagan was, history will not look upon him as a great president. During his tenure, we had record interest rates, horrible deficit spending, and a scandal called Iran Gate. But Reagan had a winsome personality, a charming manner, a keen sense of humor, a covering of Teflon, and, most important, the face of the leader.

Where does preparedness come in? Winston

Choosing to lead...

Churchill prepared his whole life for the European conflict that began in 1939. He was a Parliament back-seater who studied hard. He was made for war, and war made him.

It is too difficult to prepare in a vacuum for leadership in crisis that hopefully will never come. Former North Carolina Governor Jim Hunt prepared and worked hard for something called Smart Start to give the state's youngest children a better chance to be prepared for beginning school. He could not have prepared for the devastating, catastrophic damage of Hurricane Floyd in 1999. He dropped everything, went to the crisis-control center, and personally took charge of response. That made his governorship as much a success as did Smart Start.

What do you want to lead? What are your strengths? What are your interests and proclivities? Study those, strengthen those. Then, study the things you're weak in, and work to prepare yourself in those areas. Sometimes it works, sometimes it doesn't.

Al Gore worked his whole career to be president. He has not made it to this point, and my prediction is that he never will. He first tried at the too young age of 39. "I was never ever so glad to have a birthday," he said when he turned 40 – the age of respectability.

Gore technically was more prepared to be

president than was George W. Bush, but the mantle didn't fall on him in the contested, bitter election of 2000. The cloak of leadership by authority did not fall on President Bush either after that election. He received leadership only by position. The real mantle of leadership by authority fell on him with the collapse of the World Trade Center towers on Sept. 11, 2001.

Bush wore the mantle well. So well, in fact, that he put his reputation and prestige on the line in the mid-term election on Nov. 5, 2002.

For the first time since 1902, in an off-year election, the president's party claimed control of both the U.S. Senate and House of Representatives.

Courage is an essential element of leadership, and Bush consistently passes the test. He is a decisive wartime leader. If Bush wins re-election in 2004, one reason will be because he *chose* to lead.

You may never get the tap on the shoulder, no matter how well you are prepared. That's going to come to only a very few people. But hear this: If you're not prepared, it won't happen to you.

Billy Graham was prepared in 1949 when his Los Angeles crusade caught the eye of newspaper publisher William Randolph Hearst. When the spotlight hit, Graham was prepared with conviction of purpose, savvy in marketing, the common sense to establish financial accountability that left him untouched by scandals that rocked other national figures, and by having confidants to hold his trust. Every leader needs a trusted friend to tell him whether the emperor is wearing no clothes.

New York Mayor Rudy Giuliani will be remembered for his leadership after 9/11/01, when the man and the moment met. How any city could handle such an event with the efficiency and bravado of New York, I don't know. It has to be credited in large part to the mayor, who, until that time, was far from universally adored. His place in history is secure. All previous problems with the women in his life, police killing people, and the crackdown on street vendors will not matter. Strangely, his large success in battling organized crime as a prosecutor will fade into distant memory.

Some schools now offer a degree in leadership. I can't imagine gaining in the classroom the skills to be a leader. On the other hand, leadership is like any kind of a journey. You're always a student. You're always in school. School is never out for the professional.

#3

THE BIG IDEA

Even springs run dry if not replenished.

Chapter Three

KEEP THE LEADER REFRESHED

∼ There's no juice in a steamrolled tomato. You need to get up every day with a purpose. A lot of people don't consciously aspire to great leadership; they just want to make a living and live a life of purpose. People who do their best at whatever they do are leaders in their part of the world.

I have loved every job I've ever held. I loved being a cashier, serving with a smile. I loved dipping ice cream, and gave big scoops. I loved having a radio show as a schoolboy, spinning platters and making chatter. Your approach to work is not just an attitude; it's an ethic.

When I delivered newspapers in fifth grade, I wanted to increase circulation beyond what anyone else was increasing. It was a competition. I wasn't physically engineered for sports, but the fire of competition burned hot in me. I'm hard-wired for work. It's a drive within me that could not be programmed or educated into the circuitry. When I turned 60 in 2002, I looked back and realized that I'm still basically the same person I was at age six. Is that good? It's not good or bad; it's just the way it is.

Arguably, you cannot change your personality, and be very careful about wishing that you could.

More people are going to self-help, self-improvement courses today than ever before. We're going to any lengths to find "the answer." Is it Tai Kwan Do? Yoga? Meditation? Handball? Winter dips in icy streams? I'm looking for a magic pill to maintain a certain weight. My slender friend says the simple answer is not to eat so much. My more informed rationale says that I have a fat gene.

Consider your personality a gift. It's important to realize your gift and enhance it.

KEEPING THE LEADER IN YOU REFRESHED

If you dig into the hole, you're supposed to come up with water. If you come up with silt or sand, you're burned out. The flames are licking at your feet. What is your refreshment? What do you do to keep fueled, fresh and feverish for your work?

Do you run, read, worship, go see your child, contemplate your navel in the woods? Whatever it is that refreshes you, go to that source often, regularly. It is not a selfish act. You must stay refreshed, fueled. If you get to the point where there's nothing left, you've let down the people you lead. Imagine their terror if they come to you for something, if a crisis arises, and you have nothing to offer?

We're a strange lot, really. The overwhelming weight of our schedules becomes a source of pride.

If someone asks to see you and you can fit them in before next month, you feel you're not impressively busy enough. Look hard at your schedule, and you may see that it's filled with draining commitments and has no reservations for refreshment.

When I go to the YMCA and beat the weight machines to within an inch of their lives, I enjoy the delicious ache the next day. I enjoy it so much; then I don't do it again for a month. Why?

Don't claim you don't have time to take care of yourself. Make time on your way to work, or coming home from work. Do it first thing when you get up in the morning. Walking is the simplest, cheapest, best exercise, and you can do it anywhere you are. Make the time to refresh the leader in you.

In 1994, after 11 years of pouring myself into my job day and night, week in and week out, my trustees graciously granted me and funded a 4-month sabbatical that saved my career and probably my life. I didn't realize how really, truly, completely tired I was until I got away.

On my way to the seminary in Alexandria, VA, where I was to spend six weeks cut off from family and work so I could find the Mickey that I'd lost, I suffered an honest panic attack, the only one I've ever had. When I got there, I was overwhelmed with a hypertension attack from the sudden withdrawal of everything that identified me, that provided the external definitions to tell me who I was. I was on my way to find the internal definitions, but until I had them, losing the externals frightened me almost unto death.

My six weeks in the seminary, which were followed by several weeks overseas, were filled with testing, group dynamics, and a weekend away to a retreat setting where all the participants spilled their guts to each other. It concluded with a three-day silent retreat. No talking. We ate meals together – silently. We prepared our meals in silence. At night, one person read aloud. Then, no talking.

The purpose, of course, is to get in touch with yourself, to get in touch with God, and to experience deep rest. This structured, restricted time helped us get in touch with nature and listen to God when most of our lives are spent in offices and cars listening to ideas, complaints, issues and problems.

We took naps. Do you remember how delicious is a nap? Are you too big, too busy to pull a cover over your shoulders on Sunday afternoon and shut your eyes, waking up wondering where you are and what day it is?

Some participants couldn't stand to be alone with themselves. They couldn't stand the sound of silence. I came to relish it.

My "Aha!" came later when I had to work out my plan of action for the following year. I was required to consider and put on paper my diet, exercise and meditation plan. I was supposed to work on that for the next year, and then come back. The whole exercise shifted from mental to practical.

Today, I don't get as tired because I'm in better shape physically. If I'm in good shape physically, I can recover much quicker from exceptional periods of hard work. Do not be embarrassed to schedule your personal time. Do not wear the false pride of busyness. Retired minister-writer John Claypool has a sermon titled "Who cuts the barber's hair?" No one takes care of the leader if the leader won't take care of himself or herself.

If you need this thought to "justify" personal time for your own health, remember this: If the leader is unhealthy, it is very difficult for the organization to thrive.

#4

THE BIG IDEA

*When you care,
you'll earn the authority
of leadership.*

Chapter Four

EMBRACE YOUR STAFF AT ARM'S LENGTH

⁓ It's lonely at the top. There's only one leader. You earn your pay and prove your merit when you make those decisions that only you can make. That's why you are there.

Too many "leaders" today make decisions by attrition. They simply delay deciding until the issue resolves itself. But not to decide is to decide. If you don't put your stamp on the decision, you're leaving your staff and your organization swinging in the wind from the oak limb of coincidence and circumstance.

You're not going to be right every time. I have been wrong. And since most nonprofit organizations are about service, they are heavily personnel-oriented. So, you can guess that my wrong decisions have largely been personnel decisions.

Sometimes, the loneliness at the top can prompt a leader to become too friendly socially with the staff. While you want relationships with staff that go beyond the 8 to 5 slot, there are difficulties ahead if your best friends outside the workplace are those you supervise in the workplace.

While social conviviality may grease the

machinery in the workplace, you also may bring in problems from the outside that hinder job performance, both your own and that of co-workers. Spouses, for instance, are not operating in the same orbit. Their perceived slights in social settings may affect the gravitational pull of the workplace.

We take on a persona of different perspectives in different venues. When I'm at work, I'm a little different than when I'm home. When my wife is with me in a setting, I'm a little different. Thankfully, Kathy is a tremendous asset to me, and I can work one side of the room while she works the other. If I had to feel responsible to keep her introduced, circulating and mingling while I'm working, it would be very difficult.

A certain professional loneliness is part of the CEO job. Can I have backslapping, vacation-trip, dinner-party relationships with subordinate staff members outside of the workplace? Probably not. Such a relationship with an exclusive few will certainly foster jealousy among others. It also makes the supervisory role much more difficult.

Suppose Kathy and I went to dinner with one of my direct report staff members and the next day the staffer messed up badly. How hard would it be to take corrective action with that staffer? How hard would it be to do the right thing if the right thing is reprimand and probation – or worse? Does their social status with you make them immune from correction? I want to be friends with members of my management group, but we can't be social intimates.

A LEADER'S EXPECTATION OF STAFF

I'm an embarrassingly easy leader because I expect only one thing from my staff; simply, nothing less than their best. After you have earned the authority of leadership, and your staff sees you are giving your best, you can demand their best. If they withhold their best after you have established that as the standard in your corporate culture, they need to be cut loose. They need to have their future freed up for them.

But, most often, they aren't "freed up." They hide and you hide, and negative, under-performing personnel are left in place to drag down the work environment and infect others with their malcontent. When "your best" and "good enough" joust in the workplace arena, it is not hard to imagine which one gets dehorsed.

You might think that's too negative a perspective. It simply is true. I've realized that I cannot motivate my staff. Individuals motivate themselves. Motivation is inherent. I can inspire them, which I guess is a form of motivation, but I can't motivate them if they don't want to be motivated.

What I can do is provide an environment in which motivation can take place. Do you provide your employees the tools they need to perform their best? The environment I can provide may be a new computer, an office suite, an assistant to handle the load. That can motivate an employee to be better. I can provide training, send them off, do things for them they can't do for themselves that show that the company cares for them and that I care for them. If you feel cared for, you'll work all the harder.

On the other hand, if employees don't feel the boss cares for them, they'll get you. They'll not do it with open defiance, of course. But they'll be late, procrastinate, talk about you, talk negatively about the organization at the grocery store and barbershop. If they don't feel you care for them, they'll get you, not necessarily in a way that will bring you down but in a way that will keep you from getting your agenda accomplished.

One thing that helps employees feel secure, that helps them know you care for them, is when they sense you have a center of certainty. When they pull back the layers in crisis, in vision, in leadership, they see a rock on which they can lean, on which they can depend.

They want a leader to be spiritual, especially if your organization has a religious base. Even if it doesn't, they still want a person who is in touch with a core of rock-ribbed values.

When Malden Mills in Massachusetts was virtually destroyed by fire in 1995, owner Aaron

Feuerstein, whose grandfather founded the business, paid his workers for 90 days while the plant was being rebuilt. "I had to rebuild," Feuerstein said. "There was no way I was going to take 3000 people and throw them in the streets. And there was no way that I should be the one to condemn that community, which had suffered so much in the 20th century, to economic oblivion. No sir."

When crunch time comes, employees wonder, is the leader going to fold or is there something there to keep him going and keep us going? They need to know that you, as their leader, support and value them, that you will stand with them and make decisions in public that support that stance in private.

Once, one of our very best childcare workers was accused of neglecting a child in her care. We are hard and swift on any staff member who is neglectful. But I knew beyond doubt that this worker would cut off her arm before she would be careless with a child. I could trust her, and I stood by her. That loyalty promotes loyalty, and I have no more faithful, caring worker than this person today.

What you hope is that this kind of loyalty filters all the way through the organization. You hope the social worker knows his supervisor will stand by him, and the residence counselor knows the social worker will stand by him. And that it filters into the children we serve, that they know if they establish a pattern of honesty and hard work, their staff will trust them and stand with them through crises large and small. I would like to think when staff members see the man or woman at the top display that kind of confidence in them, that will transfer to the children and say, "You may mess up, but I'm going to be there, and stand by you."

After a new employee had been with us a few months, I called and asked her to give me a half-hour to talk. Nervous, she asked her supervisor what I wanted. The supervisor said that Dr. Blackwell just wanted to talk with her, see how things are going. That supervisor told me that when the employee left my office, she was dancing because I cared about how it was going with her.

Someone said sincerity is the key to success. When you learn to fake that, you'll have it made.

But, there is no faking genuine caring. Employees look for it in their leader. When you care, you'll earn the authority of leadership

#5

THE BIG IDEA

*If you don't learn the jungle,
the lions you thought were tame will eat
you in your tent.*

Chapter Five

LEARN THE CULTURE BEFORE IT EATS YOU

∽ Sometime after midnight in my second bewildering week as the new CEO at a statewide organization serving hundreds of children each year with a 1983 budget of $6 million dollars, I suddenly thought to myself, "What in the world am I doing here?"

For the first time in my life, I felt lost.

I was not lost in the sense that I didn't know where I was. Mine was the lostness of a typical man behind the wheel of a car in a strange neighborhood, self-denying in the face of his wife's exasperated sighs. He knows where he is; he just doesn't know how to get where he wants to go, and he will not ask directions.

I knew I was sitting in a nice leather chair in a wood-paneled office, and that it was very dark outside and very empty in the rest of the building and that I had been there 18 hours already, with no end in sight. But after trying to get my arms around the vast network of services, constituencies, employees, board members, budgets, debts and assets, facilities and clients, I realized my arms were too short. And I wondered, "What have I gotten into?"

My predecessor had taken home with him every file accumulated during his 25 years of service. For reasons known only to him, he had provided me no overlap, transitional time. So, the very first time I saw my office, I entered it as president. When I asked the president's secretary, whom I met that morning, for the files, she told me there were no files. The previous president apparently considered them his personal property and had the maintenance staff deliver them to his house.

Imagine. Because there were no files, I had no record, no history, no strategic plan for one-fourth of the institution's entire existence. There was no list of sites, facilities, employees, budgets, boards or direction in the president's office. I had to find them wherever I could.

I felt like a new coach of the Atlanta Braves who doesn't know where the locker room is and has to field a team to play the New York Yankees tomorrow. I didn't have a lineup card, didn't even know the names of the players or where to meet the bus.

Employees were sheepish and hesitant to express an opinion. Nobody wanted to do anything. They would tell me anything I asked for specifically, but nothing else. Everything I got, I got on my own. I had no help.

I began to perceive this organization as a great ocean liner that had begun to run out of fuel, but whose momentum carried it forward, albeit at

Learn the culture before it eats you

a slower and slower pace. Many passengers didn't even know it was starting to list in the water. Even fewer saw the iceberg looming at the bow.

That's not to say this was an unhappy or ineffective place. There was simply an institutional bliss, borne of a process employed for decades. The staff perceived that the next decade would be just like the previous nine, and that I would do my job well if I simply gripped the wheel and kept the ship on that course. But, in my frantic efforts to figure out at least what ocean we sailed, I'd already learned that we more resembled the Titanic than the Queen Elizabeth II.

There is a distinct advantage in naming a person from the outside to handle the helm of an older nonprofit. A person promoted to the top after long years within the system simply cannot see the need to do things differently from the way they've always been done.

If smooth leadership succession is like a relay race, we really dropped the baton. I cannot overemphasize the importance of transition. I had none. I had no relationship with my predecessor. I could never call on him for anything.

So, about midnight, I'm bone tired, my eyelids are scratching lines in my corneas, and I'm wondering if my old job will take me back. What to do? I did what I advise you to do. I called a wise old friend.

I talked two hours to a long-distance friend of many years. He was wise, a victor in many such battles. Our conversation gave form and substance to the intangible, dark mists that swarmed me. He didn't know child care any more than I did that night. But he knew how to direct my thoughts to the task at hand, and to the vision that both established the institution 98 years earlier, and that compelled me to invest myself in its next decades of service.

That long day grown into night (22 hours, 6 a.m. to 4 a.m.) was my catharsis, my turning point. It was not a lot of fun but it was giddily illuminating. I realized I knew nothing about child care, but that was OK. I knew a lot about human relations, families, education, vision and leadership. Learning about child care was the least of it. The processes, procedures and technicalities were a body of knowledge I knew I could master.

What I had, and what this organization needed, was vision and an ability to voice the vision so that the most discouraged and timid staff member could hear it and respond. But first, I had to get a grip on the organization's culture, so I became "one of them" instead of someone new trying to impose a strange template on their lives.

BE FIRMLY SEATED IN THE SADDLE BEFORE APPLYING THE SPURS

From the earliest days of "the orphanage" and

in a culture promulgated by every administration, the children's home had become very paternalistic, as was the accepted practice. All staff members were expected to live on campus, attend the campus church, and accept assignment to various campus "volunteer" activities.

In the early years, joining the staff earned you membership in the orphanage community. You lived on the grounds, ate the food. You received vegetables from the garden. You could have your personal laundry done. If you wanted to go into town you could, but you didn't have to leave the campus for anything if you didn't want to. When children went to the movies, they marched single file the mile from campus to downtown.

The culture was familial, patriarchal, and matriarchal. The previous president and his wife were very much in control of the organization, in the No. 1 and No. 2 positions. Issues that arose in social or church settings affected workplace relationships and effectiveness. Children and spousal issues became workplace issues. Church leadership was departmental leadership. Having several members of the same family as employees was encouraged.

Employees were involved in Vacation Bible School during the workday. Whole building staffs left work for Christmas open houses in other buildings. When employees left town for business meetings, sometimes their children stayed in cottages with the children in care, supervised by the staff. Some great friendships evolved from such arrangements.

Such alliances and circumstances, however, sometimes made workplace effectiveness very tenuous. In one instance, a director supervised an assistant who supervised the director's wife who supervised the assistant's wife. Imagine the difficulty of a corrective workplace action in that situation!

Because of interwoven alliances and family/workplace relationships, and because a very significant denominational support offering had just been eliminated, there was an underlying current of unease, even of fear, when I arrived. Those few in the know, which did not include me, saw a difficult era on the horizon. Change was in the air, and like wolf smell in a sheep's nostrils, change was scary.

How was I going to figure out the culture, make it work for the good of children and families, and not get eaten in the process?

Your organizational culture may chew you up and spit you out. Instead of a ravenous shark, I saw this organizational culture as a crocodile. If you let the crocodile slam its jaws shut on your leg, you're a goner. The muscles that pull the jaws closed and hold them there are very strong. But the muscles that open the jaws are comparatively weak. So, I jumped on this croc's back and wrapped my short arms around its jaws and held them closed until

I could understand and befriend it. And I didn't get eaten.

It takes courage to trade hot breaths nose to nose with the crocodile. As you wrestle during the great learning period, which may be years, you must:

- Replenish your own spirit
- Find ways to maintain objectivity
- Keep your eye on the prize.

You may know what's wrong in the culture you've entered. You may know that certain people in the culture are cancers who carry the rumors and keep the old culture alive, spreading it into new employees. But you have to bide your time.

In nonprofit organizations, you "clean house" at your own risk. Longtime employees often have cultivated friendships on the board. They have forged alliances with other employees. They wield personal power even if they've earned no positional power.

I knew I needed absolute loyalty in the positions closest to me. You will not succeed if you do not surround yourself with people who believe in your vision and who are willing to carry it out. Reassignment to legitimate other tasks is often the best way for you to begin to arrange around you a staff, which shares your vision. It didn't take me long to see that some staff members were not in positions that best suited them. When they were reassigned, they flourished and everyone benefited, including the organization. Just as beneficial, when some personnel could not accept a reassignment, they left to fulfill their futures elsewhere. And the culture slowly changed.

In my organization, a long-term employee told each new counselor "the way it really is" after the counselor had finished orientation. So, he took it upon himself to bequeath the pecking-order culture to each new employee.

This ingrained culture, if negative, can be harder to change than the stripes on a skunk. And if those saturated with it get their backs up, the stink they raise can be just as brutal.

A lot of the people at this new work wished me success. But they wanted me to succeed within the parameters of the culture they knew and that gave them comfort. They wished for my success, but they wished for it in the comfortable, familiar manner of the previous administration. I had to plant my face in that psyche in a hurry.

You must establish yourself as your organization's face (see Chapter 1). I knew I had to start immediately. First, I visited for a half-hour with every single employee at each facility statewide. Then, I conducted regional meetings across the state where our supporters and church leaders could meet the new president. We identified our constituencies and let them know I was coming with staff members to a location near them.

A lot of my college and seminary classmates were in positions of leadership by now, so I gained quick acceptance in those arenas.

You have to understand the culture you've joined before you can change it. You can't be consumed by it. If you keep your arms locked around its jaws long enough, eventually the crocodile will starve to death.

Today, 20 years later, I'm a part of the culture I've helped to create. If my successor is not used to writing, teaching, traveling constantly the breadth of the state, speaking frequently in churches, civic groups and to employee groups, he or she will have a difficult transition. If the eventual new president stays in the office all the time, he or she is going to have a hard time.

It takes years to change an organization's culture. We've had almost 100 percent turnover in administrative positions during my tenure, only a very few of which I've forced.

Today, the culture is completely different. It is a business operation, but still with a heart for children and families. It is smooth-functioning, humming like a finely-tuned engine. We've slowly but deliberately moved into a technological age. We've kept up with more needy children and more dysfunctional families while adjusting to the shift from primarily public to primarily private placements and all the differences that means in relationships and funding.

HOW DO YOU OVERCOME CULTURE AND MOVE AHEAD?

You cannot disregard the organization's tradition, its success, the good things. Celebrate the successes. Those successes are among the very things that attracted you. They will undergird you.

Remember, too, that you're not trying to make a new institution.

If a snake doesn't shed its skin when it's time, it will die. Once it sloughs the old skin, it's the same snake, but it's brighter, faster, stronger. Your organization will be the same.

Find and maintain a sense of timing. You must know when to crouch, when to pounce. You may want to pull off a scab, but make sure that you know how much you'll bleed before you do.

The leader must be the leader. This is always true, but especially true if you are joining an organization beset by recent controversy or scandal. Be the leader. Be proud of past success. Repeatedly pronounce the vision. Declare the vision at every opportunity. Communicate it precisely, repeatedly, constantly, and enthusiastically.

You must have the conviction to see that your organization's original mission is not unnecessarily changed by whims of fashion or by the flavor of the day. Although the Baptist Children's Homes mission needs constant new expression, in some ways, I'm expressing founder John Mills' original 1885 vision.

I'm chief cheerleader for that vision to care for hurting children and broken families. What is vision? It's foresight, with insight, based on hindsight. Vision is the mantra of the early 21st century. Every executive search firm asks every governing board "What do you want in a leader?" and the answer always is "personal vision."

If personal vision is so important to leadership, how do you develop yours?

#6

THE BIG IDEA

*If you're not the fastest wildebeest
in the political jungle, you better forge
some alliances.*

Chapter Six

SURVIVE YOUR POLITICAL JUNGLE

∼ Every morning the jungle lion awakes knowing that he must outrun the slowest wildebeest that day or go hungry. Every morning the wildebeest awakes, knowing that he must outrun the quickest lion or become lunch.

That keen awareness keeps both lion and wildebeest intensely alert to his surroundings. It makes them aware of the watering holes, scents in the breeze, the presence of other friends and enemies, movement in the tall grasses, the easy trails, the hiding places and the high ground. Each is aware of the alliances necessary to keep him safe.

Are they being political animals to take all these things into consideration? Of course, they don't have a logical sense of this instinctive awareness, but they know that if they are to negotiate their jungle to live another day, they had better know how to negotiate their landscape.

As a nonprofit leader you live in your own jungle. And your landscape is potentially as dangerous for your organization as any jungle is for the wildlife within it. And you must be a political animal to survive and thrive.

UpsideDown Leadership

In 1991 when a group of personal detractors was going ballistic, they accused me of being "a politician." I confess. But the political animal I am has no negative connotations to me. You'd better be a politician, too, if you understand the right context – bringing all the forces together to get your aims accomplished.

Webster's fifth definition of politics – and the one I like best – is "the total complex of relations between people in society." If you do not make every attempt to consciously navigate that "complex of relations" jungle, you're a slow wildebeest, and that glint you see is the lion's incisors about to sink into your throat.

Just think of the relational web you must negotiate in nonprofit leadership. Below are some of the strands that my residential child-care and family-services organization must traverse. Yours will intersect in many places, and you will have some unique to your organization. We must deal with:

STATE POLITICS

Certain rules and guidelines govern your operations within state government-mandated parameters. There's no way around it. But you can influence those parameters.

Often the Capitol building looks foreboding and its occupants unreachable. But that's not so. Ours is a representative government. Just as you represent those you serve, you have representatives in government at all levels. Know them, meet them, correspond with them. Make sure they know your name and are familiar with the issues you serve. That does not mean you work in their political campaigns, but more on that later.

One of North Carolina's national leadership initiatives is called Smart Start, which is basically a partnership for children. I wanted to be on Smart Start's governing board because it would be such an innovator in children's issues. I had to lobby hard for that. It sat for two years until I called a friend who I knew had the governor's ear. Manage the complex of relations.

As nonprofit leaders, we have to fight for our seat at the table. Is that political? Yes. Is it somehow demeaning or unbecoming? No. That's simply the truth of it, and if you're not leading an organization for which you're willing to trade elbows at the table with the big boys, you need to do something else.

- Department of Health and Human Services
- Departments of Social Services
- The Court System and Juvenile Justice
- Mental Health

These offices offer and shape legislation that will affect children: when a child is taken from or returned to parents, licensing standards, per diem supplements. They determine punishments and custody and facilities codes and ratios and requirements. The voice of children, from my perspective, needs to be heard in these hallways. And, if it's heard only to voice a problem, it won't be well-received.

Weigh in on issues being debated in your state legislature. You're an expert in your field. Don't leave it to non-experts to saddle you with "work rules" that will make your life miserable and your organization ineffective simply because you didn't want to be "political."

POLITICAL PARTIES

You need to work the leadership and committees of political parties. They will have influence and maybe ultimate decision authority somewhere down the line. Be careful not to be "identified" with one party or the other, however. In a two-party system, one is always "out" of power. You can't afford to be identified as a partisan of one party. If your guy loses, the rising star to which you hitched your coattail could burn you.

If you're a nonprofit, don't make political contributions. My organization makes contributions to the local hospital and school, and is very supportive of youth efforts in our areas. But you cannot safely make a contribution to a political candidate. You're treading on extremely dangerous territory, aligning yourself in a partisan fashion.

Because I'm conversant with both sides of the political aisle, I can walk with the attorney general into the governor's office and talk about things meaningful to children and families. Smart Start is an outgrowth of such conversations. To be involved like that, I have to constantly prowl my portion of the jungle with persistence, attitude and timing.

NATIONAL

As a local or statewide organization, your involvement nationally will likely be through your professional organizations and affiliations. You can't afford to be in Washington, so your professional associations employ lobbyists to work on your behalf. Be aware of that work and be ready to write a letter or make a phone call when you're alerted to an important vote.

COUNTY, CITY POLITICS

You likely will see more immediate results being politically active at this level than at any other. In what way?

Your clients probably are students at the schools and have special needs the schools are required, but reluctant, to accommodate. City or county roads go past your facility. You want them cleared of snow and kept in good repair. When you have a telephone problem, or your heat goes out, you want top priority on the repair waiting list. You want visibility in the United Way drive and allocations. When the senior adults are looking for greenway for walking and bike riding, you need to be aware of intentions they have for your vacant lot.

You want to know whether the highway commission has sights set on your land or if it's going to put an interchange over your building or condemn your facility for a new road. Does your economic development office want to build a shell building to start an industrial park on your land or adjacent to it?

You want and need to know these things before you read about them in the newspaper or get the public notice in the mail. If you don't, you will have no voice in shaping decisions and your only option will be to react to decisions that others are making for you. You cannot afford to be anonymous.

Let your local politicians know you're a part of their constituency. You're a good corporate citizen.

Contribute in ways that make up for the fact that you don't pay taxes. Make them aware of what you do in the community to contribute. We don't pay corporate taxes, but think of the number of employees who live, shop, pay taxes and use services in this community. We're a good citizen. Our employees adopted a street, committing ourselves to keep it clear of trash. When they need a tree decorated at the hospital, we contribute. We contribute an enormous amount of volunteer hours in the community. We give 10 gallons of blood to the Red Cross drive, and our staff members have led the Woman's Club, Lion's Club, Rotary and other civic organizations.

When possible, use local vendors, even to the point of buying ads in the local newspaper promotions, in your school's yearbook and football program.

We make a contribution to Communities in Schools, Thomasville Medical Center Foundation, Neighborhood Night Out. We allow groups to use our campuses as part of their route for "walks" to raise money.

DENOMINATIONAL

The institution I lead is proudly denominational, as are a great many nonprofits. Consequently, our jungle includes other humanitarian, educational institutions also doing wonderful work, and also competing for the same limited benevolent dollars we covet.

But just because you are sectarian, or religiously affiliated, don't think that you don't have to "prayerfully" scratch for each dollar that will make a difference in the lives of those you serve. Not everyone in the denominational office shares your specific concern.

My organization is Baptist. Structurally, our denomination has a "state convention" consisting of the voluntary affiliation of 4,000 churches. Almost all of those churches voluntarily align themselves with one of 80 regional "associations." So there are immediately three important constituencies of which I must be aware because each has a part in support for my organization.

Add to that the million Baptists in North Carolina who are primary donor prospects and you can see how expansive the jungle becomes.

When your denominational mother ship provides a significant amount of your funding, you must be active in the budgeting process. Don't be the short-armed boarder at the communal dinner table. Know the processes and know the people who make them work.

When you make your budget presentation, it better not be the first time you meet or talk to the budget committee members.

Some years ago, my denomination conducted a study to re-evaluate how it funded social services ministries. They proposed that I regain a statewide special offering, but it would cost me a half-million dollars in the annual budget. I needed the special offering returned, but I could not allow the dramatic operating budget hit.

They told me, "I know you'll go along with this because you're a team player." I said I wasn't going to go along with it. I couldn't. I told them on the spot it was unacceptable.

It cost me all the political capital I'd accumulated in my first six years here, but this issue had to die. I called every person on that committee. My approach was simply that such a drastic cut would hurt the children.

What I'm saying is that your nonprofit has several significant funding sources. It is imperative that you be politically astute enough to know the players, know the processes and be involved in both. If you let the processes work without you, your meal will always be that of the hyena – leftovers on the carcass – and you'll never eat with the lions.

YOUR OWN BOARD

Bring your board along with you at every step. If you are to be astute "politically" anywhere, spend that political energy here. Start immediately establishing relationships.

Early in my administration, I tried to meet my trustees on their own turf. I would spend the night in a trustee house. I'd meet them for breakfast. Because my institution is denominationally affiliated, I press upon them how important it is for me to get into their churches.

I make many, many phone calls and send many cards. One year I called all 36 board members on Thanksgiving Day. Another year I called as many as I could on either Christmas Eve or Christmas Day. I simply told them, sincerely, "I'm thankful you're a trustee at Baptist Children's Homes." When you can't be everywhere, work those phones.

It's hard to make a bad call to somebody. Even if you don't know what to say, you call and say, "I'm thinking about you."

That goes for employees as well. One time an

employee's dad died, and I happened to call right when he was praying – and crying – with his dad's friend. Afterward I heard how much my call meant to him.

They may not remember if you don't call, but they will remember if you do. They sense that you cared during a situation that might have been insignificant to you, but it's the biggest issue of their life.

I send a tremendous number of cards to various constituents – for funerals, birthdays, anniversaries. It's not just a perfunctory card, but I've developed relationships to the point where I can personalize the cards with meaningful insights.

If you don't show you care, you do so at your own peril.

Just because we are nonprofits and serve altruistically doesn't mean that every family member thinks we are the favored sons. What happens when there is an influential person in the process who just has no affinity with what you do and for your organization?

You know when you're looking at him or her, when the vote is taken, no matter what you've done, he or she is going to speak against you. What can you do?

1. Remember he is going to be there. You're not going to change him or go around him. You'll have to recognize his position.

2. Recognize her for what she is – give her her due. Recognize who you are – a leader fighting for your organization and for the benefit of those you serve.

3. Realize that he's not an "enemy." Therefore, he has no power to control your mental focus.

4. Reach out to her, include her, say nice things about her. Learn what buttons appeal to her ego, and press them.

5. Relegate other people, when it's appropriate, to deal with him.

Sometimes you'll have to go around the person. The risk is that he'll find out that you did so and make life harder for you at the next budget meeting. But you can't let a negative person roadblock your needs. If this roadblock is the top banana, befriend his board. You are constantly making other alliances.

These actions may muddy the water. That's the price of fighting for your clients and organization. Just make sure you don't burn the bridge. Time will take care of many ill feelings that may arise from honest disagreements in the family.

Just don't get down on an antagonist's level. Keep speaking, keep talking, keep lifting the mission.

If you ever go into revenge mode, you've lost because you become less of a person. As I write this, a war based on revenge rages right now between

Israel and its Palestinian neighbors. No one can win, and another generation of hate is being conceived.

I'm not a vengeful person who tries to bury somebody. But CEOs who don't bristle when their institutions are threatened – even if they're putting themselves at personal peril – need to be doing something else.

You can survive for a while in the jungle hiding under a vine, but you'll never command your jungle until you swing from that vine.

#7

THE BIG IDEA

You string a network one line at a time until you can talk to your entire universe.

Chapter Seven

COMMAND YOUR POLITICAL JUNGLE

⁓ A jungle politician keeps his nose to the winds and his ears alert. When the monkeys chatter, he wants to know why. When they fall silent, he knows the reason. When the buzzards circle, he knows the carcass they sniff and he knows if he doesn't network, that carcass may one day be his.

Lots of animals populate the jungle. Only a few command that environment. If you will be counted among the lions and elephants, know that they don't course the savanna alone.

Most nonprofits are small, with a budget under a million dollars and every day is a challenge to catch the slowest wildebeest. Networking with decision-makers and power brokers in the categories I listed in the previous chapter is essential to your survival. Most of us feel too insignificant to make a splash in the big ocean. But we're not, because what we do is important. It's important to your clients, to you, to your board, and just as important to your political entities.

How do you network to gain command of your jungle?

Consider what you have that's important to

others? How can you share it? Do you have a facility, a meeting room, rare technical equipment for video conferencing, a cook who can prepare a splendid meal, a singing group or entertainment, a funny speaker, something new? Find a way to share it.

One important, simple step is to invite. Let people know you're open to their visits. Bring the players from your complex of relations to your site.

It's important that the Baptist Convention president be familiar with what we do. I invited him for a tour when he was in the area, and we sat together and talked and he began to more fully appreciate what we do. Now when he sits in a budget committee meeting and someone says, "Baptist Children's Homes doesn't need the money," he'll be able to say, with some assurance, exactly why we do need the money.

When an issue is coming before our denominational budget committee, my development staff is in touch with committee members. I make crucial calls.

When persons are being nominated to serve as trustees on my board, I let the nominating committee know who has been interested and supportive of our work. Those are the kinds of people I want on my board, not strangers who have no particular means or interest in our mission.

I call the liaison to the nominating committee and send him copies of my books. I tell him how glad I am that he has this responsibility, and invite him and the committee chair to meet at one of our campuses.

This is not manipulative and self-serving. I'm a part of this family, and if there's anything I can do to enhance our position in the family, I want to do it.

Instead of manipulative, it is transparent, altruistic, mission-driven and necessary to let the larger family that supports you know that they're always welcome at your place. It's friend making, public relations and development. And those are functions integral to your successful leadership.

Good things have happened here, not because we just sat and thought, "Wouldn't it be nice, if..." but because we went out and made things happen.

CARVING TURF IN THE LARGER JUNGLE

It is not easy for nonprofit executives to gain a seat at the table in the larger corporate community. For-profit corporate leaders gain a place naturally and easily.

Corporate people don't run in our world for several reasons. Number one, we don't offer a return for them. Their throwing a bone our way doesn't guarantee a significant bone will be tossed their way. What does it gain our local furniture manufacturer to have the president of Baptist Children's Homes on his board? Is my "company" going to buy 10,000 chairs?

Although the education, savvy, awareness and influence level of nonprofit executives match that of our friends who operate in the for-profit world, very few corporations seek that savvy on their boards.

A second reason is that corporate people don't feel the nonprofit leader has the edge, the psychological hardness to make tough decisions. They fear we'll cave on the moral side.

On the other hand, corporate people like to get on nonprofit boards. It raises their profile, attracts business, is good for their status in town and enables them to rub shoulders with influential philanthropists.

The nonprofit executive must work harder than a corporate executive to get attention for himself or his organization. We labor in anonymity.

The media hover around people in the for-profit world. Yet as a business, my organization is larger than most. We're the oldest continually operating "business" in our community and employ 350 people statewide with a $20 million budget. Who touches as many lives in North Carolina? But, because we're a nonprofit, our impact is somehow amorphous, vaporous.

For instance, a corporate leader gains notice by position, and a $23,000 gift to a local YMCA is big, banner news. My organization receives a $600,000 gift and gains a line in business briefs.

There is no automatic, positional influence if

you're the CEO of a nonprofit. The influence you wield is only personal, gained by consistently, over time, showing yourself professional and capable.

I'm not afraid of public scrutiny or of public examination, personally or for my institution. The more you're known, the better chance you have of being understood in the public marketplace and of being able to hawk your product.

Occasionally a nonprofit executive who has paid his dues, pursued his passion, networked, trained and plied his craft can enjoy a leadership position in a group populated primarily by corporate leaders. Politics is my passion, and I've been involved in North Carolina's Institute of Political Leadership (IOPL) since 1992. IOPL is a bipartisan organization intended to help quality persons gain elected office. It's a preparation ground for people thinking of running for public office.

When a conflict arose, I was asked to mediate. Then, when the board chair resigned, I took his place.

I led the organization to survive several crises, using experience gained at a nonprofit. I helped engineer a move for the organization to gain a permanent home at the University of North Carolina at Wilmington, and gained respect. When we were faced with a leadership transition due to several retirements, I was charged with that responsibility.

Corporate execs, lawyers and professionals are looking toward me to lead them in a common pursuit. I've led a large nonprofit for decades, so it's not a surprise to me to be seen as a leader. I'm just demonstrating that the nonprofit executive carries no natural, positional leadership authority into a corporate setting. You must work for every bit of respect you gain in that forum.

My first identity is as president of Baptist Children's Homes of North Carolina. Any positive thing that happens to me happens for the benefit of Baptist Children's Homes. Any accolades enhance my agency and all of us. The wider my net is cast, the better off our agency is. The same is true for you.

It is important to be visible in your community. Working in the ranks of your local Rotary Club puts you into contact with people you need to know but would have no legitimate natural connection with if not for your common labors in the mutual organization.

HOW DO YOU DEVELOP POLITICAL ACUMEN?

Politics is not a dirty word. It's just how you get things done.

A lone wildebeest is dead meat. Working together, the herd can ward off an attack. As a "politician," you form political alliances or you're dead.

Some are born with the ability to forge relationships, and that's all political strength is – relationships. You do favors. You know when to hold and when to fold, when to call in your chips and when not.

The best way to collect political chips is to do something for somebody else before you ask them to do something for you. Call, write and befriend them when they're down. They'll eventually get through the crisis, and they may wind up in a position of power someday and they'll remember you.

Keep in mind that genuinely caring for people is not self-serving. If you leave the impression that you are just trying to earn credits for a future favor, your efforts will be self-defeating.

Your political success will depend on alliances. To survive, such as the last one remaining on television's popular "Survivor" series, you must form alliances.

It's not necessary to agree on everything, but you want an alliance on which you can depend. When votes are cast, you need to know where your ally's will fall. In true politics, your allegiance is to the party and your colleagues depend on your vote. Political majority leaders aren't called "whips" for nothing.

When you form alliances, you have to have gut assurance that they're going to be with you no matter what. When you form an alliance with your sister, you know you're a team at all costs, unless, of course, you meet her in the finals at Wimbledon.

If your alliance goes wrong, you didn't nurture

it, you didn't keep up with your ally. Deep and abiding alliances are usually deep and abiding friendships, too.

When an alliance is defeated, one of the parties may feel betrayed. Someone may sell out and betray the ally. Most of the time, people are going to look out for No. 1. In only the strongest alliances will the parties say, "If you go down, I'm going down with you."

If you're going to be in the political arena, which you are, you need the courage of your convictions. You must be bold enough to set your sails against the wind. To lobby effectively for your cause, you must be willing to:

- Stick with it.
- Enlist allies.
- Be patient because you're going to have to explain the same thing over and over again as you talk to other people.
- Know why you want the thing you're pushing for.
- Know why you're campaigning for it in the face of much resistance.
- Stay on point, on focus, in your presentations.
- Uphold the principles and ethics of your organization.
- Be well-versed and know your organization inside out and upside down.

The denominational mother ship of my organization has been in political turmoil for more than two decades. It is interesting that no one has ever asked me to take sides. This institution is viewed as apolitical. I feel like a political eunuch in some ways.

Part of me would like to be out there in the mix. But that puts the institution at risk. Everyone loves children, and the Children's Homes crosses all lines. I'd love for all parties to coalesce around us. I'm probably the only North Carolina Baptist CEO who speaks in a church with 12 in attendance one Sunday and one with 800 the next, crossing all lines, from rural to suburban, conservative to moderate, shaped-note hymnals to high church liturgies, praise song to split chancel. This free passage through political portals is hard won, and I'm not going to jeopardize it by trying to identify with a single political element.

Negotiate the entire complex of relations. It's the only way you will ever command your political jungle.

#8

THE BIG IDEA

*People resist change because they are afraid.
A good leader absorbs that fear, gives employees
a person on whom to deposit their fear
and move on.*

Chapter Eight

EMBRACE CHANGE AS YOU WOULD A RICH UNCLE

⁓ In the aftermath of the horrible terrorist attacks in New York and Washington, DC, on Sept. 11, 2001, the single, starkest realization of a shocked populace was that nothing ever would be the same again.

Everything changed.

American's world perspective changed. Our sense of safety, security and well-being changed. Gone was our illusion that everyone loved us, that we were seen universally as a benevolent big brother. Confidence shattered that our bordering oceans isolated us from the insanity inflicted upon us from terrorists overseas.

We didn't handle that realization well. Much of America's competence for the future hinged on its confidence in the future. When that confidence crumbled, competence crashed. Our stock market toppled; air travel practically ceased; the whole economy nose-dived. New York City alone lost 100,000 jobs, and 11,000 businesses tanked. To attract buyers, automobile manufacturers offered zero percent interest, and one topped that offer by adding "no payments for a year."

"Close-in" airport parking disappeared. Interminable lines appeared. A spasm of patriotic display prompted flags and flag decals to show up on millions of vehicles. American awareness of other lands increased. Our soldiers fought and died in a Middle Eastern nation few could find on a map.

Change burst into American consciousness with a furor not seen since Pearl Harbor.

But America had been changing long before 9/11/01.

Our manufacturing capacity was moving overseas; technology was changing business processes; college was becoming the minimum educational requirement for good jobs; mid-management jobs were eliminated by the tens of thousands; non-English speaking persons were filling more and more service jobs.

Change is constantly altering America, the way you live, and the way you do business. For some, change is a constant headache. For others, change is a constant challenge. For all of us, change is a constant.

Your ability to anticipate, accommodate and embrace change will determine your organization's viability into the future. Your market will change; there is no question about that. Think of the organization created to fight polio. Polio in America virtually no longer exists, except in laboratory dishes.

But the March of Dimes lives on to improve the health of babies by preventing birth defects and infant mortality.

At the turn of the 20th century, when a parent's death meant complete inability of the surviving parent to care for the family, dozens of orphanages grew to meet the need. At its population peak, Baptist Children's Homes' largest campus cared for more than 400 children. They lived about 30 to a cottage with a single matron as overseer. Children went to school half a day, and farmed the other half to raise their own food. They came at all ages but stayed until they graduated from high school, and they walked off campus wearing a new suit with a dollar in the pants' pocket.

Today, that class of children hardly exists. Medicine and peace mean that parents live longer, and there are far, far fewer orphans. If Baptist Children's Homes existed only for orphans, we could care for them in one cottage. Instead, we operate 16 facilities across North Carolina and serve some 2,000 children and their families each year in an array of services designed to meet needs that hardly existed in 1885. Today, we serve orphans of the living – children who have been abused and neglected to an extent that requires their removal for their homes. Or, their own behaviors at home make it imperative that they find temporary residence somewhere else until more acceptable behaviors can be learned.

Even in that context, we embrace change constantly. We adjust program to meet need. We make changes in personnel, technology, locations, buildings, vehicles, relationships with placement agencies and government. We approach the need for these changes as neither good nor bad. It's just change necessary to meet need.

Your challenge is to move your organization and staff to embrace the change required in a constantly fluctuating landscape.

CAN I COUNT ON YOU?

My organization's single greatest change, during my tenure since 1983, was our inclusion of "the whole family" in our services. We were born to serve orphans. When a crumbling social structure sent us children who were neglected and abused, our staff members were their strong advocates. We love, nurture, cry over and pray for all our children every day. We are like mother hens, covering those children with our protective wings.

Eventually, though, I realized that if we served only the child, we sent the child back into the dysfunctional situation from which he came. If the family did not participate, sign off on goals, have conferences with the social worker, allow a social worker into their home, then nothing would change.

One resident told me upon his discharge, "I'll

probably be back, because my mama's not going to do anything."

I started leading discussions about serving the whole family, about helping the parent realize the part he or she played in this dysfunction and helping him or her overcome it. We could offer parenting classes. Our social workers could go into the homes to observe and offer suggestions on anger management and constructive confrontation skills.

This thought met with fairly universal resistance among the staff. Our social workers were tied to the kids. They got their warm fuzzies from the kids. They didn't want to work with the "nasty awful parents." They just wanted to take the kid and save him. Alumni who came from bad-parent situations didn't like families included in our services.

Persuading for consensus is a good policy, and I operate that way most of the time. But finally, I grew weary of talking about it. At what became the final discussion on the matter, I slapped my hand to the table and said, "No more discussion. From this moment, that's the way it is."

When staff members wiped the shocked look off their faces, they went ahead and began working toward the change. What they possessed after my adamant statement that they didn't have before, was a clear mandate from the president and a certainty on how to act.

That's what your staff needs to embrace

change. When the winds howl and waves crash over the rocky shore, the sailor looks for the lighthouse, the clear and certain beacon on which to guide his course.

To be successful, anything your agency wants to do must have your endorsement as the leader. Your message of support must be clear and forceful. There is no room for ambiguity or to buck against the system, no excuse for ignorance of your wishes. Sound that note clearly, consistently and often. Take every opportunity to repeat it.

You will still have resistance because 99 percent of people fear change. Fear of change is historical and universal. Early maps showed uncharted waters populated by dragons.

People will say they want change until it becomes time for change. Bill Clinton earned election as president on the promise of change. As soon as he started to make changes, rebellion erupted. Think universal health care.

But, the clearer your signal, the less resistance you will encounter. I was fairly resistant to change myself most of my life. I am more willing to embrace change and be a change agent than I was in 1983 when I started at BCH. That's part of my own maturity and self-awareness.

Your team needs a leader with a calm center of certainty. If the leader shows anxiety, ambiguity and indecisiveness, the people will be more anxious. If

Embrace change...

you start retreating after you make the decision, your leadership eventually will be questioned and ignored.

But, hear this. Sometimes course corrections are necessary. Lead through them. That doesn't mean your original decision to change was a mistake. Maybe the path you chose to follow to embrace the necessary change is the wrong path.

Although my agency has embraced many changes in its long history, I want to share two critical changes from early in the new millennium to illustrate some ways to help you navigate those swirling waters:

- The change in the long-standing procedure for admitting children into our care;
- Adding statewide connectivity through information technology.

I've learned not to spring change on the staff. I let them know that it's coming early enough that they feel ownership in shaping it. I called my management team in individually and told them, "There's going to be change. Can I count on your support during this time of transition?"

One member said, "I hate change, but you can count on me to participate."

The one in charge of adding the technology component ran into opposition early and often. She brought her anxiety to me and said, "Let me hear from you one more time – this is going to work. We are going to put computers in the cottages and teach the kids. We are going to be connected statewide." She needed that clear note sounded again.

She said, "If you tell me something, whether I believe it or not, I can act on that."

If the leader assumes his or her role as a repository for people's fears, staff members can leave their crippling fear with their leader and move ahead. Their leader's clear, certain, confident demeanor can filter fear, uncertainty and ambiguity from the air, and they can breathe easier.

Turf issues will arise. Our whole technology effort became a separate department, and moved from under the supervision of the business office. Changing the admissions process challenged staff comfort at every level.

The admissions process addressed a fundamental change in probably the single most important piece of how we do business. Today, when a child needs a placement, he needs it now. Our admissions process was cumbersome, interminable, and put too much decision-making power into the hands of staff, which could make their own jobs easier with a few strategic denials.

Our consultant told me this change could not happen without my saying it must. He warned me

Embrace change...

to prepare for a great deal of resistance – a warning that turned out to be similar to saying that an atomic explosion might be loud.

#9

THE BIG IDEA

Your staff will embrace change when you help them understand what's in it for them.

Chapter Nine

WHEN CHANGE FOLLOWS YOU HOME, CLAIM IT

∼ Any change will draw opponents. Your job is to help your staff see two things:
 1. How the change will benefit your organization's mission, and
 2. What is in it for them?
 What is your mission, your primary business? Railroads, once the dominant shipping and travel entity in this country almost disappeared because they thought that railroading was their business. They forgot they were in the transportation business.
 I made it clear that a more streamlined process in admitting children is fundamental to carrying out our mission. Our resident population in our largest campus was down, in great part because of our cumbersome admissions policy. We can't help children who are hurting if there are no children here, if the cottages are empty. I asked them to consider the look of our field in the future. Are we going to be a part of it? I helped them see that if we don't embrace change, our field will leave us behind.

At the same time, the staff makes mission happen. I had to show our employees the benefits of the change because the ultimate measure of their acceptance is still "What's in it for me?" If they don't see benefits for them, why should they embrace a change?

Before implementing our strategic plan, I went around the state myself and explained it and explained it and explained it. After what I thought was a particularly effective presentation outlining the merits and import of the changes ahead, how our institution would move forward into the future, how we would be innovative, needs-driven and effective, a staff member stood and asked, "Yeah, but what's in it for me?"

I just sank, and so did everyone else who was involved in the process. As much as you go over it, there will be some people who don't get it. They come with preconceived notions and leave with the same preconceived notions. You can write it, and they won't read it. You can build it, and they won't come. You can say it, and they won't hear it. But keep saying it because leadership is persuasion. Your task is to persuade your people to your vision for the benefit of those you serve.

A tentative endorsement from the leader for a new policy that will change their way of doing business will not garner staff endorsement. How would soldiers attack a dug-in enemy if their leader said, "Ah, let's try to root those guys out. I think we can do it."

Don't think the only benefit your employees are looking for is a raise in pay. That's always welcomed, of course. But most employees in the nonprofit sector are called more by a sense of mission than money. Help them see that embracing the change brings them benefits such as increased competence; increased efficiency; to endure less paperwork; more safety; a better work environment; more consistent time off; higher job security, and higher contribution to the mission.

How can you get employees to understand and embrace change? State the vision – and restate it. Say it over and over and over again. Only your conviction and constant repetition of the vision will overcome the rumors that inevitably swirl up when change is in the air.

Sometimes, even that doesn't work. One employee became a de facto "expert" in an antiquated word-processing software. Other staff members called her with questions about that software. We were using a hodgepodge of applications and made a system-wide decision to get all users onto the same software. She resisted the change. She murmured that the new software wasn't as good, and she wasn't going to use it. She planted a seed of doubt and fanned the fear of change in others. Her body language left no doubt that she was resisting the change. She continued to use the old software until it was removed from her computer. She refused to see the benefit of change, and it was forced upon her.

When rumors start, they soon become "the truth" that sweeps the system. Then fear takes over. A person's first law is self-preservation. It's hard to get it across that his turf is safe, while at the same time persuading him to embrace the change. Why? Because change does alter turf.

TIMING IS EVERYTHING

Comedian Bob Hope is renowned for good timing. He could deliver a line at the right moment that made it funnier than if it had come a second earlier or later.

Sometimes the changes you make percolate for months, or even years. You know a change is necessary, but somehow, it doesn't seem the right time. Go with your gut, as long as you're just not being chicken-hearted about it.

Why do you see a problem and allow it to linger? Sometimes the timing is just not right for a change. Maybe your board chair likes that system. Maybe the staff member who created it is just a year or two from retirement and you'll avoid two years of hassle by waiting a year to push for change. Maybe you're in a period of low staff skill or morale.

We lived with our old admissions policy long enough to see that it had outlived its usefulness.

When change follows you home, claim it

After being aggravated with it long enough, the irritation started to form a pearl. I knew we needed to look it over, top to bottom, inside out, and deal with the root of the problem. Then, after too long considering that problem, we moved into advanced information technology and, suddenly, the time was right to deal with both problems.

There is no formula to know when the time is right to call down the hailstorm of fire that change brings with it. It's not kronos or chronological time. It's a kairos time – from the Greek meaning fullness of time or "ripe and ready" – when you know the pendulum may not swing back this way again. You realize it's counterproductive to do it earlier. You didn't have the push, the passion, the urge to do it at that point. Now, you do. Now, you must act.

But, what is the trigger that says "now" and not "in a minute?"

With this admissions procedure system I'm talking about, which is far more significant in our business than you likely can imagine, it hit me when I was at home thinking about it. It bore a hole in my skull. I suddenly was bone weary of talking about it.

That Sunday morning I started calling staff members across the state to form a presidential task force to tackle the issue head-on. Those I couldn't reach, I left messages for them to call me that night, no matter the time. I got my last returned call at 10:30 p.m.

I told each of them that we're doing something wrong. The need for our services is up, but our resident population doesn't reflect that. Everyone knew it. It was time to shake it up. And it was time for me to realize that no one else was going to do what I wanted done without my direct initiative.

Sometimes it's a righteous anger. You've done something one too many times. It just hits you, and you say, "We're going to fix this right now."

When I told my area directors what I was doing and what talents I needed on my team, they all volunteered. You should have heard their responses. "It's about time," they said. "Thank you for asking me to be a part of it. It's needed. I can't wait."

That approach was effective for several reasons:

1. It showed that I was aware of the problem;

2. I didn't try to put a preconceived solution on them;

3. I asked their help in arriving at a solution;

4. That request made them responsible;

5. When their recommendations were presented, the rest of the staff recognized that they came from their peers, which prompted higher buy-in.

After the team's third session, they got down to where the water hits the wheel, to the point where they are identifying the resistance, and to where they are facing the question themselves: "Can I change? Can I lead the change in my area? Can I take the heat to lead the change?"

As the executive leader, you must undergird those change agents in your organization who have caught your vision. When enthusiasm wears thin in the heat of change, just as the iron ingots turn to liquid in the furnace, you have to be there to keep things from melting down.

To bring change to your organization, you must be committed to the long haul. So many strategic or "long range" plans sit on a shelf, because leadership doesn't have the tenacity to carry them through.

OWNING CHANGE

Change is hard for everyone. As a leader, you're ahead of the curve. You've pondered the change for months, or even longer. You consider the change to be imperative and have weighed all the options you can imagine. But, as you start to tell others your ideas of change, it's brand new to them.

Be aware that when you tell someone his or her life is going to change, it's like a death. Something dies. Some way of doing things, some self-identity, some comfortable, consistent part of his life is dying. It's going away.

You give a person some time off when there's a death in the family. You let a grieving person have a few days to cry, to evaluate, to consider the future. That's kind of a neutral period. You don't assign that person a big project.

Your organization needs this neutral period,

too, when the death of "the old way" is announced. When the old way dies, give the organization some time to catch its breath. You must continue to conduct your business, but you wait to introduce initiatives.

In a sense, this neutral period is like comic relief in a horror movie. Real drama wears you out if it's ceaseless fright. A laugh, a pause in the midst of the terror lets you regroup.

During this period, be visible. You need to reassure with your presence. Tom Peters calls it "Management By Wandering Around."

This is a period in which you need to be intuitive. Have your antennae out. Be open to the accidental answer. Listen for what people are telling you beyond the words they use. Sense when their grieving has passed, or at least is not still inundating them, then move on to the new beginning.

There are always degrees of pain with change – anxiety, fear, total immobilization. In the decision process that brings change, when all the options have been discussed, all eyes still turn toward the leader, looking for a decision, a nod of the head, the "Let's roll," for their own courageous moment.

They're about to lose something. They know that for sure. You've promised that they're about to gain something, too. But that is basically unknown until they agree with you to pursue the change.

Can you give them something to replace their

perceived loss? Tell them, "Here is a better way. We are not keeping up. We're falling behind in a competitive environment. This is the direction the field is going. We're clinging to the past. We don't need to fear the future. We can do it better, more efficiently. Work with me and help me to determine the best way to implement it."

Naturally, no one wants to abandon his or her comfort zone, including you and me. But there's no growth in that zone, and I want my staff members in their growth zone, not in their comfort zone. There won't be change without some kind of pain, and people want to avoid pain, so they avoid change.

How can you get them to grasp that there is a rainbow at the end of renewal – on the other side of change?

I hope you have a history with them. It doesn't have to be two decades, but it should be a consistent history. Have you built trust by being a spiritual leader? Do your people know you have a solid core? Can they trust you? I can tell my staff, "I've been with you guys 20 years. I haven't led you down a primrose path yet. You know I'm not going to. I've been your strongest advocate." If your staff doesn't know you in that way, you may need to introduce yourself before you implement change.

Ultimately, if you don't help your organization sail bravely into the storm of change, change will overwhelm, wash over and drown it.

#10

THE BIG IDEA

*Developing resources is all about attitude.
Realize you are a joy geologist and you uncover
veins of joy when you show others how they
can positively affect lives.*

Chapter Ten

MINE SUPPORT LIKE A JOY GEOLOGIST

⁓ Many mornings, my first waking thought is some version of "Where am I going to find the $55,000 it will take to operate Baptist Children's Homes today?"

No matter what your responsibilities are as chief executive officer of your organization, they all boil down to this: You are responsible for securing the money necessary to operate your organization. You are the chief fund-raiser. You can have a development staff of 100, but when a large gift is on the line, the donor wants to deal with you.

Budget security ebbs and flows. It's always a concern, never far below my conscious thoughts. Funding streams may end or change. Potential sources must be sought and found, current sources cultivated. My per diem budget income from the state is down a million dollars this year. How am I going to make that up?

The fiscal and emotional low point for me was that year in the 1980s that hardly anyone got a raise. Only the lowest-paid staff members received an increase. One trustee told me that must never happen again, and it hasn't. But in the difficult economy of the early 21st century, there are no guarantees.

In that no-raise year, we had incredible staff buy-in all the way around because I made it clear early and repeatedly that it was a belt-tightening period. My development director was a big help, stepping up to say that his staff would support the "no raise" issue that year. His staff spent lots of time with other staff members so they could spread the positive seed.

Ultimately, though, developing funding resources for your organization is about attitude.

My friends often wonder how I can thrive in an atmosphere that requires me to ask BCH supporters to contribute to its operations. They don't understand how glad I am for the privilege of asking, and the joy I receive when supporters respond positively.

And, like most people, few of my friends understand the deep running springs of joy that flow from giving.

Studies show that people who give actually live longer, healthier lives. Preoccupied with others, their own aches and pains diminish.

Giving of themselves, either through their financial means, or gifts of presence in other people's lives, taps wells of joy otherwise thought dry.

So, when I lay the needs of hurting children

and broken families before friends who can help, I consider myself a "joy geologist." I have a map and equipment to help them dig through the crust of their lives to find the joy of giving.

The main reason people do not give, you know, is because they aren't asked. You have friends who are sitting on the sidelines with a full bag of talents, gifts, and abilities under their arms, ready to help in your family, your church, your schools, your neighborhood – if only someone would just ask them.

Think of the joy you can rain down by asking.

If people do not give because they are not asked, conversely they give first of all because they are asked. The second reason people give is for the joy of helping others. As president of BCH, I have the rare privilege of helping facilitate joy.

I encourage our development staff to see its role as joy facilitators. Every day when they come to work, they can rain unbridled joy into someone's otherwise dull, gray world by showing him how to help children and families.

Let me share briefly with you how I see the significance of development opportunities.

Development officers – joy givers – are to make friends for our institution and to tell a compelling and irresistible story. A capital campaign is an organized way to tell our story.

Development officers are to cultivate investors who will make systematic and significant gifts to

Baptist Children's Homes.

They are to aggressively maintain close and productive relationships with our church constituency across the state. These churches "adopt" us and love us still. They want to secure our well-being, as we work in the task assigned us. But like our own children, when they don't talk with us, it's difficult to meet their needs.

Our development joy givers are to ensure that our various publics get the information they need about our services, and that relations with the public are wholesome, positive and productive.

They are to work closely with our staff members so that development is seen as a part of the overall mission of Baptist Children's Homes and not as just an auxiliary.

As our development officers travel the state, talking to hundreds of people every month, I rely on them to help discover persons with potential for major leadership roles, such as trustees.

Through careful research, they are to upgrade levels of giving. Those who can give large amounts find greater joy in having a significant role in a particular project. At the same time, all donors should be considered prospects for a planned or deferred gift to help secure the future.

Joy geologists are to help facilitate a continuing dialogue between outside constituencies and the internal organization. You're not a beggar. Establish relationships with donors. Be their friend – it's OK. That way you don't feel as though you're coming hat in hand every time they see you. You're not begging on Main Street with a tin cup. You're a professional, working good in lives, helping a part of a society to which the donor belongs. Not everyone appreciates you, but some do. That donor who surfaces who does appreciate what you're doing is the one you want to cultivate.

Most significant, they, we, (me) and all of us are to help our donors experience something they cannot experience on their own – the unsurpassed joy of giving.

DEVELOPING ANNUAL SUPPORT

There are instruction manuals, consultants and other professionals to help you establish or revive your fund-raising efforts. I'm not trying to do that here. But, since raising money is such an important element of any nonprofit leader's daily life, I offer a brief outline of development elements to which you should attend.

Database – Everyone who expresses an interest in what you and your organization do should be included in your database. You cannot raise significant dollars without a cultivated, educated base of donors. You should be adding persons to this base constantly and staying in touch with them frequently. I don't mean that you should start entering phone book lists, but you want to add persons with an affinity for your organization wherever they turn up. Never receive a check or a positive letter without adding that person to your database. This base of names is simply the list of people who have expressed an interest in what you do, what your organization does. Building a database is slow work, but it is very, very important.

Software – Invest in a database software that is flexible, can handle relationships, pledge reminders, and can run a myriad of reports so you and your development officer can segment the list. You want to be able to run reports, for instance, of who contributed to a certain appeal; of your $1,000 donors over the past five years; of alumni or program recipients who are now donors; who lives in certain ZIP codes, etc. You can spend $15,000 to $20,000 fairly easily on such software. Most nonprofits can find adequate software for half of that.

Newsletter – You need to have a regular communication with your constituencies. People give you money because they believe in what you are doing and trust that you are a good steward of their precious resources. You need a regular communication with them to verify that trust. You should communicate with your entire donor base a minimum of three to four times a year. While it's important that your face be shown in the newsletter so donors can identify with leadership, it's much more important that the faces of those you serve be shown. Donors want to relate to the people their gifts serve. You should have a standardized "release" form for program participants who are pictured to sign.

Annual Report – You should send an annual report to all donors. The report can simply be several pages in your newsletter, or a separate publication. It can be the front and back of a single sheet such as that of Food Lion, a huge grocery chain. But, you need to account for your income and expenses to those who provide the funds. Accountability is the byword for nonprofits and an annual report gives evidence that you account for every dollar.

Direct Mail – Direct mail is still an effective way to raise money if your letters are compelling, if they are sent to the right people, and if they ask for a specific gift for a specific need. Too many direct-mail appeals are ineffective because they ask an anonymous "Dear Friend" for "a gift" to "help us" do whatever it is "we" are trying to do. It takes more time and money, but with computers and segmentation today, you can address donors by name, tell them a real story about a real need in real people's lives, and ask them to help you with a specific gift to meet that need. You are competing with a flood of junk mail. Pay attention to your presentation, but your most effective appeal is what you are doing to change people's lives.

Annual Giving – Once a person is a donor, you want him to consider you regularly in his philanthropic giving. You should have a program in place that appeals to him on behalf of your organization and gives him a chance to renew his support every year.

Gift Clubs – Gift clubs that recognize certain giving levels can have the positive effect of keeping donors involved and moving them toward a higher challenge. If they have given $25,000 cumulatively and are in the "Founder's Club," they may be encouraged toward a goal of joining the "President's Club." Whatever your definition, the next level is a more exclusive group that has a specific donor benefit, such as an annual banquet or a group outing or international trip with the president. These "clubs" can be effective, and their purpose is to raise donors' sights to the next level.

Capital Campaign – At some point, you're going to look around and discover that you need money for important projects that will never be covered through your annual operating budget. You'll need to gird your loins, interview some consultants, and consider a capital campaign. There is no pain like a campaign. But the benefits of a successful, well-run campaign are many. Among them:

- You raise the money you need for your special project;
- You identify and enlist donors and volunteers

who are not now high on your radar;

☙ You strengthen your current board member who realizes for the first time what it means to be a board member;

☙ You identify future board members;

☙ Your annual giving receives a boost as you raise your profile in the community;

☙ You grow and train your own development staff. If you are the development staff, you'll learn so much about raising money you'll wonder how you survived before.

It's not enough to know you need money. You must define your project in a case for support and give compelling reasons for a donor to support your campaign. Remember, a successful campaign is never about the building, or the program or project; it's always about changing lives. How is what you want to do going to change lives? That's what you are about, that's what your fund-raising efforts must focus upon.

Personal Appearances – People give to people. If you want to raise money for your organization, you must be a known entity. You cannot raise significant dollars with a letter or a phone call. You must get out of your office and into the offices or homes of people who can help you. How do you become known? Be a part of things, be a member of the groups that make things happen in your community. Every civic organization needs a program at its meetings. They need to know what you and your organization are doing to meet felt needs. Make a call, get on the program.

Note the gifts that come into your organization and make appointments to go see those people who are sending you significant gifts. A significant gift may be $50 if you're just getting started. But when you develop that person as a friend of your organization, someday he or she may be a $1,000 donor or may remember you in his or her will.

Planned Giving – Speaking of wills, you want always to raise the possibility of being remembered in a person's estate planning. The transfer of resources at that stage of life is tremendous. Some analysts say that more than a trillion dollars will be transferred upon death in just the next decade. My organization once realized $400,000 within a year after it was suggested to a friend that she add in her will the words, "I bequeath the residual to...."

Of course, there are myriad ways to make planned gifts while still living, and you should have a lawyer or accountant or broker's advice and knowledge readily available to answer questions about such things from potential donors.

Remember, when you enable a person to put intangible, cold, lifeless assets to work changing lives, you are spreading joy.

#11

THE BIG IDEA

Leadership is the art of influencing others to work willingly for your goals.

Chapter Eleven

LEADERSHIP BY THE NUMBERS

∼ By now you're probably looking for the "Yeah, but..." statement. That's often what people hear who have just explained something in laborious detail, only to be met with the furrowed brow and pursed lips of a listener who says, "Yeah, but...."

I remember shopping for a car with my teenage son. He'd cast his eye on a tired old sports model that to him looked showroom fresh. Where he saw a sleek, brown beauty, I saw a mottled old rattletrap. I knew that car was trouble, so I explained everything, helping him to see the potential pitfalls of buying that car, and the benefits of deciding on another. I told him what I knew from my personal experiences, "with my first car," and from friends' experiences and my professional knowledge.

I was great, concise, clear and persuasive. The lecture should have been recorded and played before eager graduate students in adolescent psychology. It was a masterpiece, and by the end, I was patting my own back and clearing mental shelf space for my trophy in the "Daddy Hall of Fame" that surely I had just secured.

At the end of the "dialogue," I asked Michael whether he clearly understood now the importance of leaving that car in the lot and continuing his search. He looked at me, furrowed his brow, pursed his lips and said, "Yeah, but...."

So, in case you're still as confused about the qualities of leadership and the makeup of a leader, I'm going back over things with a different bent, like I did with my son.

I've talked about leadership with sweeping motions. But some people want an ABC kind of list. I didn't create a leadership philosophy for this book. I developed a leadership philosophy over more than three decades of leading organizations into a brighter, stronger future, and I've been sharing that philosophy with you.

My personal leadership philosophy, finely tuned over the course of my career in churches, civic and political organizations, and in nonprofits, follows. I'm going to give you the whole statement, then discuss the importance and application of each element.

LEADERSHIP ACCORDING TO BLACKWELL

Leadership is the art of influencing others to work willingly for your goals. Leadership is relationship management. Leaders are not born, although innate abilities should not be discounted. Leaders are not made, although motivated individuals can be taught skills and new modalities. Rather, leaders are self-made, and the best leaders are those who lead by example. Leadership is a challenge because it involves change. Leadership is dynamic, not static; flexible, not rigid; inclusive, not exclusive. Leadership requires vision, resolve, courage, compassion and sometimes, steel-willed determination. Leadership is prophetic and redemptive, soothing and blistering, majestic and humble. Leadership comforts the afflicted and afflicts the comfortable.

And now, let's look at that statement by the numbers.

No. 1 LEADERSHIP IS . . .

...the art of influencing others to work willingly for your goals:

Much of the positive change that occurs in society occurs through the efforts of nonprofit organizations. Those who work in nonprofits often are ignited by a different set of spark plugs. What motivates people to work through nonprofits? They have their individual reasons. Some are:

1. They can identify with the goals of the organization.

2. They have a part in determining or reshaping the goals of the organization.

3. They are kept informed.

4. The organization's environment is affirming.

5. Their own needs are being met.

6. They have opportunity to express their gifts.

7. Their leader is a spiritual human being.

There are social drives and urges that motivate people, such as:

1. People are motivated to participate in something that is successful.
2. The urge for security.
3. The urge for adventure.
4. The urge for mastery. It is not enough to simply be doing something. People want to be able to do things well.
5. The urge for recognition and approval.

You can see that people are motivated to work for a variety of reasons. What you want as a leader is to motivate people to work willingly for your goals. Note that there is a difference when you add the word "willingly" after "work." How can you do that?

You can badger others to do a job. You can demand, threaten, intimidate and get the job done. But, a person persuaded against his will remains unpersuaded still. You must work to build commitment. The only way to be leader and motivator is to build it.

As the leader, building commitment means not being aloof, but being in the trenches where your soldiers can see your head and heart. I carry the torch and make enthusiasm a contagious part of all we do. Often, enthusiasm will carry the day in the face of obvious opposition.

One night, I had an idea that made me bolt

upright in bed. My staff members work at 16 facilities across the state and have strong loyalty to their location. It's sometimes difficult to help them see themselves as part of a larger whole. The idea that pulled my head from the pillow like the ghost of Jacob Marley was a statewide quality and relationship improvement initiative I called QSTQR – Quality Service Through Quality Relationships. I knew that to serve children and families across the state, Baptist Children's Homes employees needed to know and appreciate each other and the vast array of constituents we served.

I didn't have a full-blown promotional plan in mind when I announced it. But I definitely waved the banner enthusiastically, and before long, it became a part of the culture. My enthusiasm sparked employee fire that soon smoked me. They got very creative. This cottage prepared lunch for that cottage. Teams made cross-stitched QSTQR logo banners, quilts and decorations. Others made lunch for child care workers, or delivered a goodie basket to another building, or sent greenhouse plants from the farm to other sites. Many staff members made personal visits to trustees and referral sources.

The enthusiasm that employees caught and their subsequent conduct in carrying out the plan culminated in what had been my ultimate goal: to celebrate our ministry and mission in the new millennium by receiving a million-dollar offering for the institution from among its sponsoring churches in North Carolina.

We started with the end in mind. I wanted something that everybody in the system could be involved in because everyone in the system would be affected. We wanted to improve service by improving relationships and bringing an awareness to the staff that we need to change the culture in the way we do business.

No. 2 LEADERSHIP IS . . .

...relationship management.

Leadership is a relationship. Consider four major relationship variables involved in leadership: 1) characteristics of the leader, 2) attitudes, needs and other personal characteristics of followers, 3) characteristics of the organization, such as its purpose, structure and nature of the task to be performed, and 4) the social, economic and political milieu.

To lead today you must manage the complex relationship among these variables. To do that well, be open with your people, be sensitive and responsive to their needs. The human race is too crowded, pluralistic, dangerous and jumbled for us to get along without being open to futures, to changes and to others.

Like a seedling, you are planting a part of yourself into the forest of another person's life when you lead. When they know you're doing that, they will go to far lengths to return that investment and favor.

I expect a lot from my staff members, and because they know I care about them, they respond with their best. After a long period of exceptionally hard work, my right-hand staff person was at the end of her rope. Without her asking, but sensing her need, I offered her an extra week's vacation. That's simply flexibility and knowing your staff. That week was more than the employee manual specified, but she had worked far above expectations and had burned her candle short. I was aware enough to flex.

I know my staff and each trustee well enough that in a crowded meeting room, I can call any one of them to the front and talk about them, name their children, where they live, their likes and dislikes. That's managing relationships.

No. 3 LEADERS . . .

...are not born, they're not made, they're self-made.

My hero, William Friday, is a hero for an entire generation of North Carolinians. This gentle-spoken man grew up in tiny Dallas, NC, in a broken family. He was raised in poor textile community. He briefly attended Wake Forest University on scholarship, then went to North Carolina State University. After a stint in the Navy, he was a university administrator, and at age 36, was tapped to lead the three-university system, which since has grown to 16. His self-making was in the education, the risk taking, the doing it in the light of divorced parents, obstacles and poverty.

In this element of leadership, self-awareness is vital. I understand the isolation of leadership, and I realize that without a conscious effort, I could lose touch with who I really am at any period in my life. I've intentionally sought, through specific processes, the self-awareness that comes after peer evaluations and guided self-evaluation.

I'm going to let a staff member who worked closely with me during an intentional self-discovery time explain the differences she saw when I took the time away to peer into that dark well of my own being.

"Watching that growth effort, he did things I didn't understand at the time. He put himself in a dangerous position to be ripped apart in his own self-awareness and learning. Part of the security to do that came with tenure – just the length of time he's been here. He had his footing and confidence.

"He went to several self-awareness and growth opportunities. They were all different classes, seminars, retreats, executive evaluations and a sabbatical. He didn't come back a changed person, but he came back a person ready to change. I thought when he got back from sabbatical, he would be a different man. He wasn't, but he was a man ready to be different, prepared to be different.

"Then, all of a sudden, there was an incredible awakening, a high, an awareness of what was going on around him, a new love for his job and for his people, a new sense of balance.

"You find out you're not going to be destroyed in these stretching exercises. Opening yourself gives you wisdom to know when change is necessary. You can call it the Holy Spirit, you can call it God working in your life, but sometimes you just do the right thing because you're given the right thing. But there is great preparation in getting to that position."

No. 4 LEADERSHIP IS . . .

...a challenge because it involves change.

Change is absolutely the hardest thing you have to do. Smith-Corona said, "We make typewriters, and we're sticking to it." They stuck unto death. IBM almost died because it didn't believe in the personal computer.

I've devoted an earlier chapter to embracing change because change is your only constant. The only thing you can be sure of when you "lay me down to sleep" is that things will be different "before you wake."

If you would lead people to embrace change, help them discover their gaps, delete that distance between where they are and where they want to be.

Create feedback mechanisms because people won't see the gaps without feedback.

Get those who will be affected by the change involved in creating the change, participating in the process. Participation is 80 percent of smooth and effective change. The Five Wave Theory of change says that people need to be knocked over five times before they change. I'd hate to think that's true.

Your job as leader is to effect change before your organization gets smacked by that second wave.

No. 5 LEADERSHIP IS . . .

... dynamic, not static; flexible, not rigid; inclusive, not exclusive.

My style is participative, inclusive, empowering, accountable. These are the four cornerstones of our institutional culture. We begin with people who have the capacity to radiate our identity. We hire good people with Christian values, compatible with our mission and purpose. I want to see that they have a sense of mission and have demonstrated that in other areas of their lives before they come to us. That's important because this is stressful work, especially for those who are the front-line soldiers in the cottages and with families.

I care about staff members as people and am approachable when they need to share something with me, or when they need some guidance. Few arrive with all the training they need, and the changing environment means that we constantly develop and refine skills. Ongoing staff development is an integral part of working life. My management group makes sure all staff members receive information and training, and we hold our staff members accountable for using that training in their daily work.

Because we hire good people and maintain positive relationships with them, we trust one another. I let people do their jobs, allowing them to make decisions from the bottom up and have ownership for the decisions they make.

My style is inclusive. I try to give everyone opportunity to exercise their talents and abilities. In the strategic planning process and in policy development, I ask for input from those who have day-to-day experience and whose working lives will be most impacted.

The result is that people seem not to resent, reject or rebel against my leadership. Instead, they willingly do what I ask, because they know I'm their advocate and will do the same for them. This can be both awesome and a little frightening at times. The leader of BCH's work in western North Carolina once wrote me, "We really want to please you. Your approval means everything to us."

That statement humbles me, and at the same time, reminds me of the high expectations my staff has of me.

UpsideDown Leadership

No. 6 LEADERSHIP . . .

… requires vision, resolve, courage, compassion and sometimes, steel-willed determination.

A leader must see things as no one else sees them; find gold where everyone else saw only gravel. He needs to capture thoughts that race through no one else's mind, to translate the future in language of the present. Leaders solve problems.

Yet, your most important leadership function is to have a dream – a vision – that is in some way ennobling, to communicate it precisely and repeatedly, and to interpret this vision to others who can achieve it by working together. You must constantly and enthusiastically reiterate the vision. You must have the conviction to see that the original vision is not unnecessarily changed by the whims of fashion or tarnished by the immediate problems of the day. At the same time, the vision also needs constant new expression.

A secret to long-term, effective leadership is refreshment, and the secret to refreshment is not to get boxed in by ideas whose time has come and gone.

Michael Jordan, an international icon as a basketball player, was always the court leader. His vision and steel-willed determination carried the Chicago Bulls to two "three-peats." He compelled them to win by his leadership, determination and willingness to take the ball in the final, crucial moments.

The San Antonio Spurs, on the other hand, loaded with talent, lost to the Los Angeles Lakers in the 2002 NBA playoffs because in the fourth quarter, they didn't know how to win. As fourth-quarter leads in several games slipped away, you could see in their faces that they were not convinced they could pull it off. But the Lakers, even trailing late, had the confident look of winners every time down the floor, eventually going on to secure their own "three-peat" in the NBA championship series.

No. 7 LEADERSHIP IS . . .

...prophetic and redemptive, soothing and blistering, majestic and humble, comforting the afflicted and afflicting the comfortable.

To me, leadership, especially in a Christian organization, means spiritual leadership. It is up to me to hold the vision, enthusiasm, and sense of ministry for the entire institution. Spiritual matter is bigger than any one person. It's way beyond me. If I can allow the blessing that is on this ministry to flow through me and bless everyone, they can share the blessing of God. I'm a conduit, a flow-through tea bag for blessings. I am leader, guide and friend.

An inspirational leader causes people to look up.

In 1933 the nation was down. The Depression weighed heavily. Europe was restless. No good news hovered on the horizon. Then President Franklin

Roosevelt delivered a radio address in which he declared that things would be getting better soon. I'm not sure where he got his evidence. But the people needed an encouraging word, and a good leader discovered a way to lift their sights. Across the nation, people who were hanging their heads in defeat started looking up again.

When a pair of reporters too inexperienced to realize what they were doing unfairly blistered my organization, my staff was down and angry. Residents were hurt. They needed my presence to assure them things would be getting better soon. We weathered that storm internally with great strength and resolve because leadership did not run and hide to lick wounds. Instead, my team and I were immediately and prominently applying healing salve to wounded soldiers.

Those are the seven elements of my personal leadership philosophy. I share them because they've been effective for the organizations I've led, and I believe they will work for you.

#12

THE BIG IDEA

The world is divided into champions and quitters. When you TAP the MVP within yourself, you will be among the champions.

Chapter Twelve

TAP THE MVP WITHIN YOU

⁓ One of the dark secrets shared by many people thrust into leadership is the doubt that they can do the job. Deep down, considering all the responsibilities, organizational issues, staff problems, financial challenges and client demands, they wonder whether they are up to it. Psychologists tell us that even many very accomplished leaders subconsciously fear that one day they'll be discovered as frauds – the Impostor Syndrome – that people will learn they haven't been leaders at all but just had enough sense to get into the boat at high tide and ride the wave.

Whether or not you share that fear, I want to encourage you with six words combined into two acronyms that will help you meet the challenges of leadership.

We all know that the biggest contributor to a team's success is the Most Valuable Player, the MVP. Let me continue that thought, but assign different words to those letters. Three characteristics a person needs to be a leader are Mission, Vision and Passion. A person consumed by these elements will be a strong leader; he or she can't help it.

Your mission defines who you are, what you are about. It sets your focus and declares your reason to exist. You should be able concisely to declare your mission and print it on the front of a T-shirt or the side of a coffee mug.

If you are not clear about your mission, you don't really have something distinct to propel you through your day. You don't have a guiding purpose to gather resources and to do your work. You don't know if your leadership is effective and if your organization is accomplishing anything. Your mission is that beacon toward which you steer. It is the purpose for which your organization exists.

Often your expression of that mission changes with circumstances. The Baptist Children's Homes mission is "helping hurting children ... healing broken families." When we began ministry in 1885, we were an orphanage. Today, we're residential care for youth and developmentally disabled adults, wilderness camping, model day care, maternity care, in-home family services, preparation for adult living. Our mission is the same, our expression has changed.

As a leader, you bring your vision to your organization's mission. Your most important leadership function is to have a dream – a vision – that is in some way ennobling, to communicate it precisely and repeatedly, and to interpret the vision to others who work together to achieve it.

You must constantly and enthusiastically reiterate the vision. You must have the conviction to see that the original vision is not unnecessarily changed by the whims of fashion or tarnished by the immediate problems of the day. At the same time, the vision also needs constant new expression.

If your organization's mission is the beacon by which you steer, your vision is the ability to see things illuminated by that beacon that no one else sees. It is your ability to translate possibilities into reality.

Your compulsion to do this is your passion. Passion is the prime ingredient to leadership. You can have a vision, but if you don't have passion for it, the vision goes nowhere. A passion for the mission allows you to be so focused on the mission that you set distracting things aside. Your passion is your joy, your fire in the belly. It's what makes you look forward to Monday.

Jimmy Carter was the Georgia governor with no national following when he ran for president in 1976. The Watergate backlash sent a peanut farmer to the White House. President Carter is a bright man of highest integrity, but he could not communicate his passion for the job and get the country through crippling inflation.

Now on an even wider stage, Carter may be the most knowledgeable man in the world on the world. And he's as gutsy as they come. He introduced "human rights" into the international vernacular. He went to Cuba in 2002 when our government didn't want him to go to Cuba. When he spoke to Cubans, he addressed them in their own language. President Carter is never going to be a super, dynamic speaker. But his passion for people, human rights, democracy and peace has made him acknowledged by many as the best ex-president we've ever had. In fact, he was awarded the Nobel Peace Prize in October 2002.

What is your passion? What claims your heart? What do you put other things aside to do?

The arrival of my first grandchild gave me a new passion. I'd heard about that consuming passion all my life. Until you experience it, you really can't know what it's like. When I talk about my grandchild in a public forum, as I relate that child to my taste of immortality or to my commitment to make her world a better place to live, I find out how extraordinarily powerful that is to people.

Which landscape would you rather drive through – one that is colorless or filled with color? The dullest landscape is colorless. A person with no passion is a colorless landscape.

People who lead lives of quiet desperation are those without a passion.

Comedian Jerry Seinfeld had a top hit television show "about nothing" for nine years, but he always considered himself primarily a stand-up comic. He turned down $100 million for a tenth season, because, he said, "This is who I am. Stand-up comedy is what I do."

Have you settled into a role? Is what you do your passion – or is it just a living?

When Los Angeles Lakers basketball center Shaquille O'Neal plays with passion, he's unstoppable. When he plays without passion, he's closer to ordinary.

Sometimes passion is more prevalent before the goal is reached. Achieving the goal dilutes the passion. If you can find your passion in the daily challenge, in fulfillment of mission, then you're got it all.

My own passion is in improving the human condition, holding my hands under the life of a child already discarded by many. Then, showing that child that he or she has potential and promise, and doing what I can to bring that potential into reality.

I have the passion to communicate an idea, to convince others that there is a better way. They don't have to be stuck in a rut and repeat the same old processes. They can let go of whatever fear keeps them ground-bound.

I'm passionate about helping people who will allow me to help them reach their potential, and I'm passionate about reaching my own potential. There are larger, broader audiences to reach. I've entertained notions of political office or directing a national agency. But then I come back and think that this is the plot of earth I've been given, and I'm doing a pretty good job of cultivating this piece of ground. Thousands of kids have come through since I've been here, and their roots are nourished. I've helped set up an apparatus through which they can be touched and healed by professionals in a way that gives great potential and meaning to their lives. A leader needs a healthy ego, but don't let your ego dictate that you can find fulfillment only on a larger stage.

Passion is the fire in the belly that makes things happen. Passion is Martin Luther standing trial as a heretic in the 16th century, declaring, "Here I stand, I can do no other."

Mission and vision can be carried out only by passion.

So, your MVP, the part of you that brings team success, is Mission, Vision, Passion. How do you get that MVP into the big game?

TAPPING THE M V P IN YOURSELF

I liked the childhood game "Duck, Duck, Goose." Participants sat in a large circle and one child walked quickly around the outside of the circle, saying, "Duck, duck..." until she tapped one child on the head and shouted, "Goose!" That child then jumped to his feet and ran around the circle in the opposite direction, trying to beat the tapper back to the vacant spot in the circle. Until the sitting child was tapped, he was really only watching the game.

You don't want to watch – you want to be playing, to run around that circle, to get a chance to be the MVP and lead your team. You want to tap the MVP potential within you. We've discussed the MVP, now let's talk about the TAP.

To me, the world is divided into two kinds of people: those who divide the world into two kinds of people, and those who don't. No, really, I see everyone as either a champion or a quitter. The ultimate question becomes: "Which do you choose to be?"

It is no shame to be knocked down. Many fighters get knocked down before winning. Abraham Lincoln is notorious for the number of times he lost bids for elective office before he became president. The shame is in laying your head on the mat and staying down.

I have never met a person who wants to be a quitter. We all want to succeed, but sometimes we get derailed. Here are three words with awesome power to help you TAP the MVP within you – Timing, Attitude, Persistence.

First is timing. Life is a challenge. But, life is an adventure, too, and it has many rewards for those who take advantage of opportunities life presents.

One of the great prayers of good timing is

familiar to most of us: "God grant me the serenity to accept the things I cannot change, the courage to change the things I can, and the wisdom to know the difference."

A champion knows how to seize opportunities and how to tie a ribbon around every day. The brass ring may come around only a few times in your life. You need to reach out and grab it. Fortunes are made, wars are won, loves are captured when someone senses the timing, weighs the risks, considers the rewards and "goes for it."

Life without risk is a life of sheer boredom. Quitters will look back with regrets in their yearbook of life and say "why," while champions always look ahead and say "why not?" The preacher in Ecclesiastes is right: "Whatever thy hand findeth to do, do it with thy might." (Ecc. 9:10)

Too many people stop growing at an early age. They go to their graves with their music still unsung, their poetry yet unwritten. Between the City of Reality and the City of Dreams, they get off at the Town of Compromise and lead lives of boredom, dullness and frustration.

The second word in TAP is attitude. It's trite but true: a champion takes a lemon and makes lemonade…and then opens a lemonade stand. A champion comes to the end of his rope, ties a knot and hangs on. A champion keeps his integrity. A champion keeps her purpose, her direction.

Minor tribulations become major when approached with a bad attitude. When you exhibit the attitude that you truly enjoy people, you appreciate that your clients and problems are opportunities yet discovered, you are an asset to your organization. Attitude is everything in dealing with people and problems. Think how often you've been through the grocery line and come face to face with a clerk who obviously didn't want to be helping you. Attitude is everything.

When I graduated from high school, a top-ranked television show was "Bonanza" and starred Michael Landon. Later, Landon starred in "Little House on the Prairie" and "Highway to Heaven." He died in 1991 of inoperable cancer of the pancreas and liver. However, his amazing, positive attitude encouraged and inspired many people. Landon said you can't do anything if you just stand in a corner. That's what I mean about positive mental attitude.

In the Chinese language is a symbol or a word that means both danger and opportunity. In context, the word can mean crisis or possibility. That's the way life is. If you view life as an opportunity for fulfillment and service, that becomes a self-fulfilling prophecy. If you view life as crisis or danger, then that will become the measure by which you live. It all depends on your attitude.

I challenge you to see life as adventure, as opportunity, as something to celebrate. The purpose of life, said writer and scholar Leo Rosten, is not to be happy – but to matter, to be productive, to be useful, to have it make a difference that you lived at all.

Finally, persistence. I've told you one of my heroes is Winston Churchill, the greatest war leader Great Britain ever had. During the dark days of World War II when Adolf Hitler's war machine was running roughshod over Europe, it was Winston Churchill who kept England's hopes alive by his determination, inspiration and rhetoric. The British were carried to fight on the wings of his words. Winston Churchill was made for war.

At the height of his leadership, he delivered one of the most dramatic speeches ever – and one of the shortest. Called upon to inspire his nation, Churchill shuffled to the microphone, raised that big head of his, paused, and said to his enraptured audience: "Never give in...never give in...never...never...never."

With that, this living legend ambled back to his seat and plopped down. The crowd sat in stunned silence before rising as one to give him a thunderous ovation.

Persistence. Never give in.

Persistence has been a key to the success of the Baptist Children's Homes of North Carolina, and persistence will be a key in the future. Persistence has brought every successful leader to his or her pinnacle. Persistence is the stuff of which champions are made.

Before Lance Armstrong won his first Tour de France, the world's greatest bicycle race, he almost died of cancer. He resolved to fight the cancer as he would any opponent trying to overtake him on a mountain climb. He conquered the cancer, and with sheer persistence trained himself into such outstanding physical condition that, at this writing, he has won four consecutive Tours de France (1999-2002) and is so dominant that his opponents admit to racing for second place.

In the great race of your life, would you be so dominant that your opponents admit second place is their best hope? Then persist.

*You can turn
your organization right side up!*

Conclusion

SOAR INTO THE FACE OF GATHERING CLOUDS

∽ As I write these final words, the world is much changed from when I conceived the first.

New York's World Trade Center crumbled, and its fiery dust has settled a blanket of insecurity over the entire world. Less than 17 months later, on February 1, 2003 – in yet another national tragedy – America's psyche took a terrible blow when the NASA Space Shuttle Columbia broke apart, killing all seven astronauts. September 11, 2001 and February 1, 2003 are the bookends for this book – ***UpsideDown Leadership***.

During the same period of time, trillions of dollars in stock value have evaporated from portfolios on Wall Street and have devastated personal retirement accounts. Golden years are turning to brass. Nonprofit organizations have seen contributions and investment revenues drop dramatically, and many have had to reduce services and dismiss employees.

In the jungle of our lives, storms loom.

On one hand, this atmosphere makes it more difficult to operate a nonprofit organization.

Donors are less certain of their own finances; foundations' available distributions are down; government agencies' chronically short staffs shrink, leaving the gaps ever wider for families to fall through; discouraging headlines make us wonder whether we're making any progress.

On the other hand, the need has never been greater for your organization, and mine, to achieve our missions in the lives of children, families, the dispossessed, the most vulnerable of our society.

If that is going to happen, if your team is going to win your battle, you must lead them. In times like these they need a sure, clear, loud trumpet sound. They need to see your face among them, to hear encouraging words, to have the vision clearly and surely repeated to them time and again in various ways.

This is no time to crouch in your den, rue the wind and tremble over dark clouds. Instead, it's a time to roar into the storm, prowl your turf, and let your pride of cubs see you strong and sure.

Your confidence will be contagious. Your team will rule the jungle. The faint will peer from behind their shelters and take heart. Those who hurt will find healing.

May you find that the gathering clouds bring not destruction and devastation, but, in fact, pour out refreshing rain.

Lead on!

About the Author

Dr. Michael C. Blackwell, a writer, public speaker, and president/CEO of one of the largest nonprofit organizations in his home state of North Carolina, is making his leadership philosophy transparent to help thousands of other leaders who find themselves in charge but aren't sure which way to go. He has been a radio and television journalist, a newspaper reporter, and a pastor.

On Blackwell's own first day in the office he now occupies, he discovered that files from the previous quarter century of the organization were gone. Now in charge of a century old institution, he felt like a new coach who didn't have a player roster. Like the Titanic, this institution's momentum was grinding to a halt, but no one on deck seemed aware of the leaking hull.

Since then, Blackwell has turned the institution right side up; put it on solid financial ground; greatly expanded facilities, programs and the number of children served; and attracted an outstanding and capable staff.